THE HIGH-PERFORMANCE TEAMS SERIES

VOLUME 1

FIRST TEAM

EVERYTHING YOU NEED TO KNOW TO START A TEAM ... LEAD A TEAM ... AND BE A TEAM

COMPILED BY THE EDITORS OF *TEAMWORK*

Writer: David Dee

Conceptual Photography by: Arthur Tress

DARTNELL is a publisher serving the world of business with book manuals, newsletters and bulletins, and training materials for executives, managers, supervisors, salespeople, financial officials, personnel executives, and office employees. Dartnell also produces management and sales training videos and audiocassettes, publishes many useful business forms, and many of its materials and films are available in languages other than Engiish. Dartnell, established in 1917, serves the world's business community. For details, catalogs, and product information write:

THE DARTNELL CORPORATION
4660 N Ravenswood Ave
Chicago, IL 60640-4595, U.S.A.
or phone (800) 621-5463 in U.S. and Canada

Dartnell Training Limited
125 High Holborn
London, England
WCLV 6QA
or phone 011-44-071-404-1585

Copyright 1995 in the United States, Canada, and Britain by
THE DARTNELL CORPORATION
Library of Congress Catalog Card Number: 95-68479
ISBN 0-85013-234-7

Printed in the United States of America by the
Dartnell Press, Chicago, IL 60640-4595

CONTENTS — PAGE

PART II
SUCCESSFUL TEAM PLAYERS

CHAPTER 4. WHAT MAKES A GOOD TEAM PLAYER?

CHAPTER 10. SPARKING TEAM CREATIVITY 159

INTRODUCTION

Dear team member:

In 1989, a major U.S. manufacturing company changed the way it had been doing business for nearly 100 years. Out went its highly bureaucratic, traditional work hierarchy. In came self-managed work teams.

When a reporter asked the president of the company why such a major overhaul was in order, the president offered this simple two-word reply: "Teamwork works."

It is a lesson that business after business has been learning since the early 1980s. At that time, industries like autos and steel were taking a harsh beating from the competition in Japan. U.S. executives, bruised by their losses, finally stopped and asked, "What do they know that we don't?"

That's when the U.S. had its first look at Quality Circles — a people-oriented management style that brings employees together to solve problems as a team.

U.S. industries quickly embraced the concept, utilizing Quality Circles and other types of teams to meet specific needs. In 1994, the revolution was nearly complete: 91 percent of *Fortune* 1,000 companies reported that they use some form of work teams.

So, chances are, today you are the member of a team. It may be a permanent, high-powered, self-managed work team, or a special-purpose team that meets only long enough to tackle a particular problem. But whatever type of team you belong to, this book was written with you in mind.

First Team is the first of three volumes in the "High-Performance Teams Series" by Dartnell. Each is geared toward helping you become a happier and more productive member of your work team.

In this volume, we explore some of the basics of teamwork.

In Part I, we look at what makes teamwork work (Chapter 1) and show some of the basic procedures and skills needed to launch your new team (Chapters 2 and 3).

Part II (Chapters 4–7) looks at the specific skills *you* need to be a top-notch team player, including how to work well with other team members (Chapters 5 and 6) and how to handle problems when they arise.

Part III (Chapters 8-10) offers tips for team leaders. But even if you aren't currently the leader of your team, we hope you'll give these pages your attention. After all, one of the basic tenets of teamwork is that leadership is shared by every member. This section can help prepare you for the day you're asked to lead your team.

In this convenient size, there's no reason you can't keep your copy of *First Team* in a handy location at your desk or work area. We hope you'll pick it up frequently throughout the day, whether it's to uncover a new tip or technique, or to test your skills by taking one of the personal quizzes at the end of each chapter.

No matter how you use it, we hope you have as much fun reading *First Team* as we did producing it. Let us know what you think. Fax us in care of "The High Performance Teams Series" at 312-561-4842. We'd love to hear the teamwork tips you've developed over the years so we can include them in a future edition!

— The Editors

HOW TO USE
THE HIGH-PERFORMANCE TEAMS SERIES

VOLUME 1: FIRST TEAM: EVERYTHING YOU
NEED TO KNOW TO START A TEAM ... LEAD
A TEAM ... AND BE A TEAM

Topics include: What makes teamwork work? ... Getting started ... Team building ... What makes a good team player? ... Team dynamics ... Working together ... Handling conflicts ... Motivating the troops ... Making meetings work ... Sparking creativity and celebrating success.

VOLUME 2: ONE-ON-ONE: WHERE THE
REAL WORK IN TEAMWORK GETS DONE

Topics include: Strengthening communication ... Motivating yourself and others ... Personal conflicts ... Handling stress ... Building cooperation ... Resolving team problems ... Getting along outside your team ... Working well with other teams ... Success with internal and external customers.

VOLUME 3: ULTRA TEAMS: UNLOCKING THE SECRETS
OF THE NEW TEAMWORK-QUALITY CONNECTION

Topics include: Tips for veteran teams ... Battling complacency ... Self-empowerment ... Taking it over the top... Training and maintenance for high-performance teams ... Customer service ... A commitment to quality ... Ethics and values and your team ... Handling transitions.

Though the topics covered in each volume are different, what you will find in each include:

- *Practical tips* and *suggestions* to help you gain more self-fulfillment and satisfaction on your team;

- *Case studies* of successful teams and team leaders; and

- *Anecdotes* and *motivational quotes* ... *Personal quizzes* ... and *Quick Tips* that you can put to work immediately.

Dartnell's "High-Performance Teams Series" has been prepared by the editors of the Dartnell team-building newsletters: *Teamwork, Team Leader, Quality 1st, Working Together,* and *Getting Along.*

PART I

TEAM LAUNCH

CHAPTER 1

WHAT MAKES TEAMWORK WORK?

"The power of the waterfall is nothing but a lot of drips working together."

— ANONYMOUS

Smooth-running teams make teamwork look so easy. But that can be deceiving. Teamwork takes work.

UNDERSTANDING TEAM PSYCHOLOGY

You're worried about your team. After an initial period of high energy and productivity, the team seems to have reached a low point. Efforts are at a standstill, and nobody seems to be enjoying themselves. Creativity is down as a result. How can you mix in a little pleasure with your labor?

It may be too early to worry. Just like individuals, teams work through various psychological stages. That's a normal team process, says Kenneth Blanchard, Ph.D., author of the best-selling book *One Minute Manager*. He told *Quality Circles Journal* that team members should be conscious of the various stages of development so they can accept them as a normal part of the team-building process.

Here are the four most prominent stages a team goes through:

1. Orientation. At this stage, excitement is high and the team is ready to charge ahead.

2. Dissatisfaction. After that initial rush of energy, the team becomes more realistic about the demands, responsibilities, and obligations of teamwork, which can lead to dissatisfaction.

3. Resolution. At this stage, the team has worked through dissatisfaction and now is joined together in a cohesive group.

4. Production. The team settles in to perform the task it was assigned.

Work teams can fail, Blanchard says, when team members are not prepared to experience the different stages. Too many teams give up during the dissatisfaction stage and never accomplish their goal. So hang in there!

'TEAM PLAYER' RATED TOP WORKPLACE VALUE

A recent survey of 125 companies in 34 industries reveals that employers rate "team player" as the No. 1 workplace value.

The study was conducted by Challenger, Gray & Christmas, Inc., an international outplacement firm located in Chicago.

Nearly 40 percent of the bosses and managers surveyed ranked "team player" as top among seven desirable work traits. Moreover, 80 percent chose it as either first, second, or third.

According to those surveyed, employees between the ages of 30 and 40 are most likely to possess the best teamwork skills.

The other traits covered in the survey were: "self-starter," "dependable," "company-focused," "responsible," "adaptable," and "likable."

James E. Challenger, president of the firm, observes: "Increasing worldwide competition makes it mandatory for companies to obtain all the value they can from their employees. This is reflected in the fact that 'team player' was named as the top workplace value."

INSPIRATIONAL

TEAMWORK: BECAUSE WE CAN'T DO IT ALONE

We have always tended to revere the airplane pilot who did it alone and the country doctor who never left the bedside. Such spirit of independence served us well and caused us all to grow tall.

But we'd never have made it to the moon without a spirit of *interdependence*. And we'd never have eradicated typhoid and smallpox and polio without cooperative effort.

We've found that no person alone can fetch oil from beneath an ocean. We have found that we are becoming increasingly interdependent — not only in our country, but also all around the world.

The spirit of interdependence will not cost more than it is worth. On the steep slope ahead, holding hands is necessary. And it just might be we can learn to enjoy it.

— **PAUL HARVEY**

HERE'S WHAT MAKES TEAMS SUCCEED

A study of 26 major corporations, summarized in *Personnel Journal*, found five specific characteristics of effective teamwork. Does your team have these key elements?

1. Probing questions that get to the point. Other teams fail because they've never identified the real problem they need to resolve.

2. Leaders who encourage creativity. Team members know that, even if an idea is rejected or modified, they are free to pose original and creative approaches, without criticism.

3. Wide-ranging debate that explores every proposed alternative, no matter how harebrained. Properly used, brainstorming is one technique that can lead to more creative solutions to problems.

4. Systematic critiques so team members can learn from their mistakes. Regular reviews of projects in a positive atmosphere of mutual learning will lead to higher-quality work.

5. An explanation of the group's decision to those whose cooperation is needed. Effective teamwork extends outside the group. When you've developed a course of action, you need to work successfully with others to put it into effect.

SUCCESS DEPENDS ON
'CARE AND FEEDING' OF TEAM

It had to happen.

Since the early 1980s when organizations first began evolving away from the traditional workplace, the media and an array of industry and service leaders have sung the praises of work teams and the concept of teamwork.

Companies by the masses abandoned traditional work practices and embraced the work team concept. In fact, 68 percent of the *Fortune* 1,000 companies now report using self-managed or high-performance work teams.

So the backlash was inevitable.

Magazine articles with titles like "The Team Trouble that Won't Go Away" *(Trainer)* began sounding the alarm bells. In "The Trouble with Teams," *Fortune* magazine reports "a growing unease" and "a worry that [teams] ... might even turn around and bite you."

But don't sound the death knell for teamwork just yet! Even the biggest cynics cannot overlook the fact that work teams *do* produce results:

• Scores of service companies, including Federal Express and IDS, have boosted productivity by as much as 40 percent since adopting work teams. David Swanson, a Procter & Gamble senior vice president, said recently that P&G plants with work teams were "30 to 40 percent more productive than their traditional counterparts."

• Smaller companies report equally positive results. Johnsonville Foods, a sausage manufacturer in Sheboygan, Wisconsin, claims productivity improved 50 percent since implementing teams.

If there is a "problem" with teams, experts agree, it's not that the philosophy of teamwork is flawed. "It's that there are a lot of obstacles," says Eileen Appelbaum, author of *The New American Workplace* (ILR Press).

Fortune magazine says when teams don't succeed, it's often because the wrong type of team was formed for the wrong purpose, or there was not complete support for the team concept.

"It's easy to spot the companies where teams won't succeed," says Joan Chesterton, team consultant. "They're the ones that have no real commitment from the top. You can't just put up posters and hand out buttons."

In fact, if there is consensus among experts, it is that successful teams spend time and energy on "the care and feeding" of their team.

Such teams thrive because members constantly work at working together. They understand what Edward Lawler, of The Center for Effective Organization at the University of California, means when he says, "People are naive about how easy it is to create a team. Teams are the Ferraris of work design ... high performance but also high maintenance."

Team consultant Suzanne Zoglio, Ph.D., agrees. She has studied high-performance teams and what makes them succeed and has compiled the results in her book, *Teams at Work* (Tower Hill Press).

"The trouble with teams," Zoglio says, "is that they are so busy *producing* they don't take the time they should to look at their own processes, to refuel, and to reevaluate their goals. If a team wants to succeed, it has to stop and reflect, 'What impact is this team having on the organization? What impact is it having on me?'"

WINNING TEAMS LEARN FROM THE PROS

The late Vince Lombardi once divulged his formula for winning in football: "Build with your team a feeling of oneness, of dependence on one another, and of strength derived from unity in the pursuit of your objective."

James L. Lundy takes 12 principles of sports teamwork and applies them to the workplace in *T.E.A.M.S.: Together Each Achieves More Success* (Dartnell). These are his fundamentals:

1. Know your objectives. Lundy asks: "Will your game strategy be conservative or calculated to 'go for broke' at every opportunity? If you don't know your objectives and priorities, how can you maximize your effectiveness?"

2. Study the rules. Every game has rules, and each team must follow them. Your task is to thoroughly understand your organization's policies, procedures, and practices.

3. Learn what's expected. You and your peers must clarify your individual roles. What does your employer expect of you? How can you measure the quality of your performance?

4. Understand your position. Define your individual position on the team. But, when a teammate drops the ball, be there to help. "Sensitivity will help the team to develop cohesiveness and consistent effectiveness," Lundy says.

5. Practice, practice, practice. Every sports team needs pre-season and between-games practice sessions. In the workplace, teams handle challenges by anticipating them.

6. Maintain self-discipline. Basketball players learn to aim before they shoot. Similarly, your team must have the discipline to do what's difficult and important instead of what's fun and easy.

7. Develop talent. "The process of analyzing needs, recruiting candidates, and sorting the eagles from the turkeys is one in which most sports-oriented organizations consistently outperform their competitors," says Lundy.

8. Welcome new teammates. On some teams, longtime members regard newcomers as threats to their security. Eradicate this attitude by finding out how each member's talents can help the entire team.

9. Coach constructively. When you see a teammate who is faltering, lend a hand. "The true team player," Lundy observes, "helps others avoid embarrassment, learn from mistakes, and build progress out of tests of abilities."

10. Assess your strengths and weaknesses. Sports teams review game films to study patterns of successful and losing team play. At meetings, discuss your flaws and find solutions.

11. Give guidance. You'll probably lose some teammates through job offers or dismissals. As they leave, try to steer them in a positive career direction.

12. Make principled decisions. Says Lundy: "Each day, ask yourself: 'Have I considered the needs of all my teammates? Do I believe in what I'm doing, or must I try to justify it?'"

Lombardi and other great coaches have created winners by following these rules. If your team does the same, there's a championship in your future, too.

'THERE ARE NO CRUMBS IN THE FOREST TO GUIDE YOU'

When the concept of teamwork is introduced to a workplace, high expectations abound from both management and employees.

But be patient, advises consultant Joan Chesterton, an associate professor in the Department of Technology and Engineering at Purdue University. "It takes time for a group of people who are put together to begin working as a team," she says.

In addition to teaching, Chesterton consults for industries throughout the Midwest.

Q. Let's say I've always worked independently. Then my organization forms teams. What one piece of advice would you offer me?

A. Speak up to other team members when something is bugging you. Nothing surprised me more when I began working with teams than the need for better negotiation and conflict-resolution skills.

Q. What advice would you have for the team as a whole?

A. It's very important that a team take as much time as possible early on defining the various roles of the team. Know who does what. If you understand your responsibility on the team, there's less chance for misunderstandings.

Q. Everything you're saying comes down to communication.

A. Exactly. That extends to outside the team as well. For example, if your plant operates on more than one shift, who on the team is responsible for intershift communication? The team should decide that.

Q. In general, is it difficult for workers to accept the change that comes with becoming a team?

A. It's tough for everyone. In general, workers are fascinated, but initially cynical. They have to feel confident that the change is real and permanent. Management has to show total commitment to the team concept.

Q. What can you tell new work teams to ease their concerns?

A. I try to give them a realistic idea of what to expect. They must accept that, by forming a team, they're venturing into some uncharted territory. There are no crumbs in the forest to guide you. They're likely to feel frightened, liberated, confused, and fascinated by the process. Sometimes they will share progress, sometimes confusion.

Q. What else?

A. Anticipate that there will be immense rewards — but not at first. It takes time. I keep a sign on my refrigerator to remind me to keep progress in perspective. It says: "Everything takes five years." Above all else, be patient.

WHAT IS TEAMWORK? SPELL IT OUT!

What does teamwork really mean?

James L. Lundy spells it out in *T.E.A.M.S.: Together Each Achieves More Success* (Dartnell):

The purpose of an organization is to achieve overall effectiveness rather than to focus on individual triumphs.

Everybody, the great novelist Leo Tolstoy once wrote, wants to change humanity — but nobody wants to change personally. We must strive to support each other.

Anybody can be dedicated to hard work and feel good about that. The vital issue is how much we can contribute to team and organizational goals.

Management has many challenges. One of the most important is to broaden everyone's vision beyond the scope of their own team.

We will never be better as a company until we are better to each other. Leaders must seek to convert individual engines into high-powered vehicles roaring ahead toward team progress.

Opportunities to assist one another are everywhere. Leaders should always ask how their teammates are doing and what they themselves can do to help.

Real teamwork is so gratifying that it may be a sufficient reward. Even so, team members who can communicate and coordinate are the most desirable assets.

Knowledge of where your team and organization are headed is critical to group spirit and success.

EXPECT THINGS TO BE DIFFERENT

Working on a team requires that members give up elements of their work environment they may have grown accustomed to. Be prepared to lose the following, says *Self-Directed Work Teams: The New American Challenge* (Irwin):

• **Someone to blame.** The team is responsible for its project and accomplishments. The buck can no longer be passed up or across company structures when problems arise.

• **Status symbols.** As team members, you are working together as equals. There's no room for special treatment.

• **The safety of hierarchical bureaucracy.** The drastic change from a hierarchy to a team where everyone is equal can be uncomfortable for some people. Self-direction brings with it more responsibility and pressure.

• **Beliefs about how people work.** Concepts such as "People are motivated toward rewards only if they will receive individual recognition," and "People need supervision to do good work" cannot be enforced in a team structure.

SEVEN KEYS TO TEAM SUCCESS

Consulting with various work groups over the years, author Suzanne Zoglio has learned that while there are many factors that contribute to the effectiveness of teams, high-performance teams share certain traits."

Zoglio has compiled those traits in the book, *Teams at Work: Seven Keys to Success* (Tower Hill Press):

- **Commitment.** Put aside personal goals for the good of the team. Focus on the team's purpose, clarify your own purpose and values, and consider how your values fit with the team's.

- **Contribution.** Create an atmosphere where every member feels included and empowered. Assess how each teammate contributes and supports the contributions of others.

- **Communication.** Create an environment in which all members feel comfortable saying what they think, whether they are asking for help, sharing new or unpopular ideas, or admitting mistakes. Encourage the team to make good communication a priority.

- **Cooperation.** Create an environment where team members handle their own assignments, volunteer to help each other, and solicit feedback from colleagues.

- **Conflict Management.** Accept that conflict is normal but learn to resolve disagreements and build trust. Set team ground rules (such as time guidelines and courtesy rules) to apply when conflict erupts.

- **Change Management.** Deal with workplace and team changes. Discuss recent changes, think more openly about potential benefits, and create an environment in the team for innovation.

• **Connections.** Work successfully with other teams to develop a positive work climate. Strengthen relationships within your team and develop relationships with other teams.

"Once your group focuses on ways of supporting other departments, you will be surprised by how many ideas you generate," says Zoglio. "And when you start strengthening your relationships with other groups, you will be amazed by how much support comes *back* to your team."

ASPIRE TO 'HIGH-PERFORMANCE TEAM' STATUS

At a recent conference of the Association of Quality and Participation (AQP), three work teams were selected from a field of 18 semifinalists to be honored for their outstanding contributions to their organizations.

A team doesn't become a high-performance team overnight. But by understanding what makes these teams stand out, your team members can aspire to become a high-performance team as well.

What characteristics do these teams share? This is the question that Mary Ellen Collins, Ph.D., president of People Power Consulting Service in Maineville, Ohio, has devoted much research to answering.

"Most teams are really just working groups — people who get together and share information," Collins told seminar attendees at the AQP conference. "High-performance teams share a commitment to goals, *and to each other.*"

Based on her in-depth study of four AQP award-winning teams, Collins has identified five common characteristics of high-performance teams (HPTs). Does your team meet these standards? High-performance teams:

1. Demonstrate behaviors similar to a religion or an elite club. HPTs have an intimate socialization process. They often share a special language — using codes and nicknames — that only team members understand.

Members of HPTs also develop a strong sense of loyalty, much like family members exhibit. "Just like a family member often takes the stance that 'I can say what I want about my family, but no one else is allowed to criticize it,' so, too, does a member of a high-performance team develop that same sense of defending his or her team and its members," says Collins.

2. Receive significant support from their organizations. Companies that have a strong commitment to employee involvement, quality processes, and overall training often foster highly successful teams. This supportive environment gives members the freedom to fail without fear of retribution. There can be no risk taking — and thus no innovation — without the freedom to make mistakes.

3. Act as agents of change. "All high-performance teams I studied were pioneers," states Collins. "They tackled issues that had plagued organizations for long periods of time. As a result, in many cases, HPTs were able to solve problems that management had tried unsuccessfully to change for years."

4. Wield tremendous influence, both inside and outside their organizations. Members of HPTs earn reputations as people to be respected. They become sought-after sources for input and action. This influence often extends into their families and communities. For example, many team members Collins studied had created mission statements for their families to follow.

5. Become vehicles for involvement and leadership. Collins reports that several members of her subject teams went on to management. "High-performance teams often become a proving ground for many employees who wouldn't otherwise get the chance to show their stuff," says Collins.

ELITISTS NOT WELCOME!

To be successful, a team must:

1. Be empowered to carry out decisions and initiatives.

2. Gain enough support from the members of the organization to move ahead.

3. Avoid becoming an elite group.

"Many times in trying to facilitate the success of a new team," says *Executive Edge*, "all the push is toward supporting the new team. While the team has to attract new members to be successful, it also must avoid becoming an elite group that excludes the majority of workers that it affects."

QUICK TIPS

- **Know the difference.** Are you a member of a *team* or work group? Compare these differences: A work group has one leader, while members of a team share leadership roles. In a work group, there is individual accountability; in a team, members share accountability.

- **Spell teamwork with three C's.** Want to help your team succeed? Keep in mind these three crucial C's: Communication, Cooperation, and Commitment. Together, they spell teamwork.

- **Safety circles.** If you perform the same type of work as others in your plant, form a safety circle. OSHA recommends such teams meet on a regular basis to identify, analyze, and recommend solutions to safety concerns.

- **Teamwork in a nutshell.** All teamwork comes down to a few simple rules, says Denis Waitley in his book *The Joy of Working* (Ballantine). They include: valuing to the others in your team, making others feel important, finding something nice to say, and listening and providing your full attention when others speak.

- **Ask for help.** Don't be afraid to ask for help when you've got more work than you can handle or you could use creative input from your team. Learning how to ask for help is as valuable a team-building skill as knowing how to offer help.

TEAMMATES COUNT ON COMMITMENTS

"A fellow team member said he could no longer trust me after I missed a deadline. That hurt! I think I'm generally trustworthy."

— J.T.R., Chicago, IL

Your teammates need to know they can count on you. They are apt to judge your trustworthiness through how well you honor your commitments. This quiz will help you rate yourself.

1. I _____ assign deadlines to any commitments I make.
   A. always B. usually C. sometimes D. rarely

2. I _____ put commitments in writing to remind myself.
   A. always B. usually C. sometimes D. rarely

3. When a peer asks me to commit to a project, I feel _____.
   A. pressured B. confused C. honored

4. If I doubt I can keep a proposed commitment, I _____.
   A. don't make it B. stall C. explain why, if I must

5. Before making a commitment to a teammate, I _____.
   A. think it through B. leave myself an out C. get my boss to decide for me

6. I _____ take any commitments I make to others seriously.
   A. always B. usually C. sometimes D. rarely

7. When I haven't been able to honor a commitment, I _____.
   A. forget about it B. always learn something C. blame others or outside circumstances to save face

8. The kind of commitments I like to make are _____
   A. the ones that make me look good B. the ones I feel I can meet C. none; I try to avoid commitments if possible

9. If I fail to keep a promise, I _____ find a way to make it up.
   A. always B. usually C. sometimes D. rarely

10. I _____ feel bad when I break a promise to a teammate.
    A. always B. usually C. sometimes D. rarely

YOUR COMMITMENT TO COMMITMENT: Give yourself two points for the following: 1-A; 2-A; 3-C; 4-A; 5-A; 6-A; 7-B; 8-B; 9-A or B; 10-A. Give yourself one point for these selected answers: 4-C;

5-B. 16–20 means that you handle commitments well; 13–15 is good; and 12 is average. Below 12 suggests that your teammates might feel they cannot count on you.

CHAPTER 2

GREAT STARTS!

"Nothing would get done at all if a man waited until he could do something so well that no one could find fault with it!"

— CARDINAL JOHN HENRY NEWMAN

OK, so now you're part of a team.
Where do you go from here?

TEAM LIAISON SERVES AS TEAM AMBASSADOR

You were recently assigned to be a team liaison. You are supposed to facilitate communication between the team and management. But you don't know specifically how you're supposed to do this.

A team liaison is more than just a messenger from management to the team and back again. He or she is an observer, facilitator, and resource — but not a member of the team or the team leader. A liaison works with the team, the team leader, and management to create an open, effective team environment.

James A. Tompkins, Ph.D., author of *The Winning Manufacturing* newsletter, gives several examples:

• In support of the team leader, a liaison ensures that the team meets regularly, manages conflict by seeking out opposing viewpoints, identifies team training opportunities, and generally ensures that the team is moving in the right direction.

• At first, a liaison attends all team meetings. But, as the team becomes more self-sufficient, the liaison need only check with the team leader periodically to ensure that the team is continuously improving.

• When attending team meetings, the liaison job fosters an environment for listening by being an active listener and a cheerleader as appropriate.

• A liaison reports to management on the team's successes, problems, and status. In this function, the liaison is not a "tattletale" but a communicator, who makes certain that the team gets the recognition it deserves and the support it needs.

• Through that open line to management, the liaison helps the team create quality goals and work recommendations that will fit into management's plan and improve chances for acceptance. In many cases, the liaison will communicate these goals from the team to management and then carry feedback from management back to the team.

An effective liaison can create a successful team environment in which members' accomplishments meet management's needs. Think of yourself as your organization's team ambassador.

TRANSITION CAN BE TOUGH

How do you go about transforming a work group from being manager-led to being team-led? Here are three clues:

1. Share information. Share what you know about company or team goals, marketing strategies, competitors, and any other element of your organization that affects the team. Encourage your teammates to do the same. A broader base of information and understanding about that information is critical to thinking strategically about the business.

2. Share responsibilities. Initially, sharing team responsibilities starts with cross training, which allows flexibility in scheduling work and enables teammates to fill in for one another. This helps to create a sense of interdependency among members, which is imperative for good teamwork. Beyond that cross training moves team members away from specialized jobs to broader responsibilities. This improves both your value to the organization as well as your ability to act in ways that are in the best interests of the team and the organization.

For example, at the Levi sewing plant in Murphy, North Carolina, team workers are cross trained in 36 tasks. They are also empowered to run the plant — from organizing supplies to setting production goals to making personnel policy.

Similarly, at Edy's Grand Ice Cream, cross-functional teams consist of four or five people who actually make the ice cream, plus a packaging operator, an engineer, a shipper, a maintenance person, and others. Each team is responsible for everything — quality and sanitation checks, meeting individual business goals, internal scheduling and discipline, training and career development.

Once teammates can do the same tasks, they are a step closer to being able to take on the job of managing the team's work. Management functions can then be rotated or shared, and the group can start to address traditional management tasks, such as planning, budgeting, and solving problems.

3. Share benefits. As you move from being individual contributors to team players, don't forget to share the rewards as well as the work. Group rewards promote cooperation rather than competition among members and reinforce that vital "We're all in this together."

Have a group celebration that recognizes everyone who helped to achieve a team goal. When everyone is rewarded, there is little reason for people not to work together.

SETTING GOALS? TALK TO CUSTOMERS!

To be worth the effort, team goals must be in sync with those of the customers.

Often work teams fail because their goals are not what the customer wants and needs, says *Boardroom Reports*.

And no wonder. Many so-called great products crash and burn because no one buys them. A product — or goal — is only as great as the need for it.

"Work teams should always function in constant consultation with those for whom they are providing their service," notes the publication.

It's up to you to decide what form that consultation should take. Surveys, complaint forms, follow-up calls, and suggestion programs are just a few of the ways to monitor the needs of your customers — both internal and external.

But one of the most effective methods for gauging which goals are important to customers is by listening. Customers know what they want. And the only way you will too is by opening your ears. Simply ask: "How can we better meet your needs?" You'll be surprised at how much information that one question, followed by active listening, can garner.

NAME THAT TEAM!

When Lisa Carlisle came home from work and announced, "Today I became a member of the LEGGS team," her husband assumed she had joined the company jogging team.

He was surprised to learn that LEGGS was actually the name of the work team Lisa had just joined. LEGGS, he learned, was an acronym for *Learning Efficiency Generates Good Secretaries.*

Like the LEGGS team, many groups have a sense of humor about their team name. But according to author Ralph Barra, in his book *Putting Quality Circles to Work* (McGraw-Hill), team members shouldn't underestimate the importance of a team name: "The name guarantees an undying recognition of achievements of that circle and connotes somewhat the personality and character of the team."

Among the team names Barra has seen: TIPS (Technicians in Problem Solving); PIP (Purchasing Improvement People); QUICK (Quality Unit Is the Customer's Key); and RIM (Recognize, Investigate, Motivate).

Selecting a team name is also important because it usually is one of the first decisions the members of a team make together. A wise team leader will suggest at the first or second meeting of the team that the group select a name. This often breaks the ice among members who still are not totally at ease with each other, especially when humorous names are suggested.

WHY ARE WE HERE?

Philosophers throughout time have asked such existential questions as *Why are we here?* But that question has a special meaning for newly formed teams.

Teams get off to a bad start when they themselves don't spell out the team's purpose and the short-term goals needed to achieve that purpose.

How does a team's purpose differ from its goals?

The team's purpose is the overall reason the team exists ("to improve customer service"). Goals are the short-term actions the team must carry out to fulfill its purpose ("answer every call within three rings").

Even established teams should periodically review the team's overall purpose to ensure that the team is on track.

Try this simple exercise: Each team member, including the team leader, writes down his or her statement of the team's mission. Then each statement is discussed to see if the team agrees on its objective.

Scale down the wording of your missions to a few concise words, such as: "to maximize profit" or "to implement Project A."

GOAL NO. 1: SETTING GOALS!

Once your team has been formed, a top priority should be to set goals: the short-term actions that the team must carry out to fulfill its overall purpose (such as saving money, cutting waste, developing a new product).

In the book *Teamwork: Involving People in Quality and Productivity Improvement* (Unipub), Charles Aubrey explains that your goals should have these goals:

- **Be specific.** A goal can be useful only if it specifies what is to be done and when.

- **Be measurable.** "Goals are intended to be a yardstick," says Aubrey. They help evaluate the team's progress. That can only be done if goals allow progress to be measured in a specific way.

- **Be results-centered.** In determining goals, concentrate on the results, not on the activities to accomplish them.

- **Be realistic.** In its early stages, a team can make the mistake of being too optimistic about how soon results may be attainable. In the end, that will hurt a project because deadlines will be missed, work will fall behind, and enthusiasm will lag. "Realistic goals are goals that are within the bounds of the team setting them," says the author.

- **Be challenging.** You'll want your goals to be realistic, but you should also make them slightly difficult to reach. "Setting aims high can motivate the team to achieve," he says.

GETTING THE JOB DONE

The team is in place and there is a project you must tackle. Simply calling meetings and hoping for the best won't get the work done. Follow these no-nonsense rules adapted from *Effective Project Planning and Management: Getting the Job Done* (Prentice-Hall):

1. Set a clear goal for your project. Make it specific.

2. Determine the project objectives. Each member should have specific short-term objectives that all point to the overall project goal.

3. Establish checkpoints. Don't let the project wander off in different directions. Checkpoints help to keep the project on track.

4. Draw a picture of your project schedule. List activities and when they need to be carried out. This visual aid keeps the project in focus.

5. Work together as a team. Teamwork is the glue that holds the individual efforts together.

6. Cheer each other. Through mutual support, help each other through the highs and lows.

7. Keep everyone informed. Post deadlines and meeting times.

8. Make the most of conflicts. Build from common ground and focus on issues, not personalities — the "what" of a problem, not the "who."

9. Empower yourself. Each person has expertise. Use it!

10. Take risks and be creative. Project teams should look for ways to make breakthroughs. Look for the new and untried approach.

LET A 'WRITTEN CODE OF BEHAVIOR' GUIDE YOUR TEAM

Throughout our lives, we learn to be competitive both in school and in the job market. Then, some of us find ourselves in the much different world of organizational teamwork. The transition can be difficult.

Author Marvin Weisbord puts it this way: "Teamwork is the quintessential contradiction of a society grounded in individual achievement."

Nevertheless, there are behavioral guidelines that you and your teammates must follow if you're going to get along and be productive.

Deborah Harrington-Mackin, author of *The Team Building Tool Kit* (AMACOM), observes: "Teamwork places tremendous demands on interpersonal skills. It requires open, honest, direct communication; the ability to surface issues and resolve conflicts; and an understanding of your own and others' feelings.

"It's not uncommon for about 20 or 30 percent of the employees involved in teams to struggle and resist the demands that they change their behaviors. Some eventually grow dramatically and achieve tremendous results; others end up finding jobs in more traditional environments."

Early in the team-forming process, Harrington-Mackin stresses, members must determine which behaviors will and won't be tolerated. This may require trial and error. Without rules of workplace conduct, damaging personality clashes are likely to develop.

The author recommends that each team draw up a written code of behavior. It should spell out common expectations, enhance team self-management, and help new members to know what's expected.

These are the basics of acceptable team behavior you might want to consider including in your team's code of behavior:

- Making "I" statements such as "I feel," "I think," and "I need";

- Listening actively to promote two-way communication;

- Respecting others' needs, feelings, and rights through civilized disagreement; and

- Sharing information and expertise.

By contrast, these are some of the behaviors guaranteed to create team dissension:

- Refusing to set aside personal agendas and work with the rest of the team;

- Intimidating teammates by arguing that a situation is an "always" or a "never";

- Displaying a negative attitude toward change, people, and the entire team-building process;

- Showing a drive to be an individual star rather than a member of a work unit in which everyone is regarded as equal; and

- Judging others quickly but being slow to examine one's own behavior.

"Team building requires that we change our assumptions about people," Harrington-Mackin says. "Often, the rules of traditional organizations suggest that employees will be dishonest, steal, show disrespect, cheat, and satisfy only their own needs.

"In a team-building culture, people must be viewed as honest, straightforward, kind, and eager to do the right thing."

PRINCIPLES — NOT RULES —
SHOULD LEAD YOU

A high-involvement company manages not by rules, but by *principles*, say the coauthors of *Leading Teams* (Irwin): "The resulting trust allows team members, with your coaching, to adapt or devise the most effective guidelines for day-to-day operations."

John H. Zenger, Ed Musselwhite, Kathleen Hurson, and Craig Perrin identify these five principles to build trust within your team:

1. Focus on issues, not people. When a team leader operates with a "Who's at fault?" attitude, team spirit is dying. Solution: Stick to issues.

Do this and, "the people who work for you will recognize that you support them," says Thelma Inkson, nursing manager at the University of Alberta Hospitals.

2. Build self-confidence and self-esteem. Self-confident people speak up, take risks, and give the team their best efforts.

John F. Welch, Jr., chairman and CEO of General Electric, observes: "We defined self-confidence as the catalyst that would release the ideas and energy we craved when we initiated a series of New England-style town meetings."

3. Nourish positive relationships. As organizations streamline, old lines of authority fade. People must find new ways to communicate.

Even goverrnment is changing. In Windsor, Connecticut, Town Manager Al Ilg organized teams for white- and blue-collar workers alike. "In government," he explains, "the word 'customer' was rarely heard. We've been around since 1633, and we just started using it."

4. Make *everything* better. "If it ain't broke, don't fix it," isn't relevant today. Every process can be improved.

"Getting team members to 'stop, look, and listen' is central to your new role," says Karen Gideon, vice president of Amex Life. "As leader, you must teach and continually urge your team to make things better."

5. Lead by example. It's your most powerful trust-building tool. Through your performance, your teammates will respond to changes, new responsibilities, and the necessity to communicate.

Subaru-Isuzu Group Leader Karen Olson-Vermillion ties the five principles together: "It takes a long time to build up trust. If you don't tell the team something that they need to know you destroy that."

Good team members make
Good team leaders

What skills make a good team leader?

Gisele Richardson, of Richardson Management Associates, which assists companies in building teams, told *Boardroom Reports* that the most important skill a team leader can have is the ability to bring out the best in colleagues.

Richardson says the skills that make an effective team leader are not much different than those that make good team members.

Team leaders should:

- Be quick to develop the trust of their fellow employees.
- Assume that team members are responsible and competent.
- Be eager to learn new skills.
- Have a clear sense of what's right and what's wrong.
- Give clear directions.
- Be generous in praising good performance.

QUICK TIPS

- **Record team goals.** When you have a team meeting to establish goals, tape the discussion. Playing it back from time to time can spark new ideas that target those goals.

- **Do you have a mission?** In Andersen Consulting's *Outlook* magazine, corporate consultant Peter Drucker says that what workers want more of on the job is not empowerment or responsibilities, but a clear sense of their mission. If you don't know your team's mission, make it *your* mission to find out and put your team's efforts in the right place.

- **Organize for less stress.** You can reduce stress by being organized, says Michael LeBoeuf in *Working Smart* (Warner Books). He suggests: Keep only one project on your desk at a time, keep items off your desk until you're ready to use them; and put completed items in your "out" basket and send them on their way.

- **No nitpicking.** When communicating one-on-one, avoid embarrassing others by correcting them, especially about minor facts. Concentrate on understanding the main point being made.

- **Presentation pointers.** You have a presentation to make to your team members. How do you hold their attention? Begin by getting everyone to concentrate on a prop, slide, chart, or other visuals that they can focus their attention on, suggests Joseph Quattrini in *Successful Business Presentations*.

HOW INVITING IS YOUR WELCOME?

"When new people join our team, it seems to take them longer than it should to fit in. Are we providing sufficient orientation?"

— **J.T.K. Mountain View, CA**

It can be difficult to assimilate information in a short time. Team members may put up barriers, consciously or unconsciously, to orientation. To see how much you help new teammates succeed, take the following quiz, based on a guide by James L. Lundy in *T.E.A.M.S.: Together Each Achieves More Success* (Dartnell).

		YES	NO
1.	Do you clarify the team's goals, resources, and expected performance and results?	❏	❏
2.	Is team building stressed to newcomers?	❏	❏
3.	Are they introduced to everyone with whom they'll be working?	❏	❏
4.	Do you clearly outline team policies, procedures, and standards of ethics?	❏	❏
5.	Is there a tour given of your workplace?	❏	❏
6.	Does a supervisor review such matters as overtime rules, incentives, and benefits?	❏	❏
7.	Are newcomers given copies of team handbooks, procedure manuals, and other basics?	❏	❏
8.	Do you frequently ask new teammates if they have any questions or requests?	❏	❏
9.	If they get off to a good start, do you comment on it and provide encouragement?	❏	❏
10.	Do you invite new members to participate in team social activities, like group lunches?	❏	❏

TOTAL NUMBER OF **YES** ANSWERS _____

YOUR WELCOME RATING: A perfect score of 10 YES responses is essential for creating a friendly environment for new teammates. Remember how you felt as a team novice and how much a friendly face and good source of information helped.

CHAPTER 3

BUILDING A BETTER TEAM

"My passion comes from backing people's efforts, getting them what they need to do the job, educating them, and working with them as a member of the team."

— BILL EATON, LEVI STRAUSS EXECUTIVE COMMITTEE

Communication and cooperation are the blocks
upon which teamwork is built.

BUILDING TRUST

You've just joined a team. Other members don't yet seem to trust you. How can you prove that you're trustworthy?

The trust that makes a team strong isn't something that just happens — it has to be built up over time.

You can help by following these six steps suggested by Robert Rogers, chief operating officer for Development Dimensions International, Inc.:

1. Maintain each other's self-esteem. Encourage your teammates when they are down. Point out how they fit into the big picture.

2. Support and praise each other. One of the best ways to encourage peers to rely on you is to ask for help yourself.

3. Keep sensitive information confidential. How can teammates trust you if you can't keep a secret?

4. Stand up for each other. Let others know that your team stands together in success and failure.

5. Avoid gossip and unfair criticism. If you earn a reputation as a gossip, your team will never share anything with you.

6. Appreciate each other's differences. Each member makes up a separate and equally important part of the team.

TAG TEAM MEALS

After a long day at the office, who wants to think about preparing dinner?

Five coworkers in Rochester, New York, decided that they didn't, so they formed a "supper club."

Each weeknight one member of the group cooks dinner for the other families and delivers it to their homes, reports *Working*

Mother. They trade off so that four nights per week each woman is the recipient of a home-cooked meal.

The five women meet every two weeks to plan menus and discuss the success — or failure — of past meals.

The women have discovered that it's less stressful to cook a big meal one night a week than to cook different meals each night. Another benefit: Because each dinner has a $30 cap on it, weekly grocery bills have been dramatically reduced.

TEAMWORK LESSON IN NATURE

Have you ever stopped to wonder why migrating geese fly in formation?

When they fly in a 'V,' the flap of each goose's wings creates an aerodynamic lift for the bird flying behind. Thus, the flock achieves about 70 percent more flying range than if each goose were to fly alone.

In the same way, coworkers who share a common sense of purpose and direction can get where they want to go faster and easier by providing help to one another. That is, by working as a team and flying in formation.

HOW YOU (YES, *YOU*) CAN BUILD TEAM SPIRIT

Just as a winning team spirit is *shared* by an entire team, the whole team should share in *creating* that positive spirit. Try these tips:

• **Find a reason for working together.** Think of how the success of the team project will benefit you personally in some way. What is it about the team goal that will bring you personal satisfaction? Help others discover the answers for themselves.

• **Care about and support your teammates.** Fellow team members may withdraw and leave participation to others if they don't feel they are an integral part of the process. Encourage participation of others. Listen to their suggestions.

• **Have determination and commitment.** For a team effort to succeed, members need to feel that the group goal is important and that their success together is as important as success separately on any individual project they would be working on.

Don't wait for the leader of your team to take action, help by taking the first steps yourself!

HELP YOUR TEAM THROUGH ROUGH TIMES

Researchers who study small-group work teams have found there are three critical periods.

By watching for these difficult stages, you can help your team weather the rough spots:

1. Orientation. During this period, members are uneasy around each other. There may be long moments of silence, and everyone is careful not to say anything that might offend.

Suggestion: Help the team through this phase by being especially friendly. Wisely used, humor can help. The most successful type relates directly to the situation. Once the initial tension is broken, researchers say, team members begin focusing on the task at hand. Conversation begins, questions flow, and the group starts concentrating on the problem it is to solve.

2. Conflict. During the conflict stage, disagreement over how to solve the problem at hand and other issues may emerge.

Suggestion: Ride out the conflict stage. It is an important part of the team process. Properly handled, conflict can help stimulate the flow of ideas, but you'll want to keep it from causing the group to disintegrate.

3. Disappointment. The group has made it through the early rough spots. The level of communication increases and the group is excited about accomplishing the task.

The disappointment hits when team members suddenly face reality: there is much work to be done. It may mean long hours of research, interviews to back up ideas, and a lot of additional thinking to implement them.

Suggestion: Be aware that this phase is a normal part of the team process. As a team member, you can help prepare yourself and others by reminding the group at the appropriate time that disappointment can come. When it does, take a deep breath — then dig in and work your way to success and a feeling of accomplishment.

TAKE THIS TEAM CHECKUP

Compare the following characteristics of successful and unsuccessful teams and then take action to make your team a winner.

Successful teams: Meet regularly, and there is a purpose to meeting. *Unsuccessful teams*: Do not meet regularly, due to physical differences (located in different plants or departments), inadequate resources, or lack of support from management or members.

Successful teams: Set goals and objectives. *Unsuccessful teams*: Struggle by without direction. If there are goals, few members are aware of them.

Successful teams: Ensure that each member has clearly defined roles and responsibilities that do not overlap. *Unsuccessful teams*: Drift. Duties are poorly defined, no clear leader is identified, and responsibility is avoided.

Successful teams: Make decisions by consensus. *Unsuccessful teams*: React to crises, rather than anticipate problems and solutions. One person may dominate, and points are debated but rarely resolved.

Six key team-building roles

Members of any smoothly operating team take on different roles that contribute to the attainment of both short-term and long-range objectives.

Thomas L. Quick, author of *Successful Team Building* (AMACOM), cites seven such functions:

1. Supporting. If you really want to support another member of your team, Quick says, you must go beyond simply reinforcing his or her point of view only when you agree with it.

It's actually more important to furnish backing and encouragement when you're not in agreement.

2. Confronting. "There are times when a person's behavior is detrimental to the success of the team," Quick explains. "Another team member may confront the undesirable actions.

"Confrontation is constructive when it's confined to people's behavior. When it involves another's personality or presumed motives, the outcome is usually one of disruption and resentment."

3. Gatekeeping. On almost every team, a few members are assertive while others may be somewhat reticent. As a consequence, certain ideas and opinions are pushed ahead too forcefully.

A gatekeeper must emerge. An effective approach: "You folks have expressed yourselves quite clearly. Now, let's hear what some of the others have to say."

4. Mediating. A dispute can become so intense that the teammates who are slugging it out no longer listen or respond to each other. None will budge. At this point, an impartial member must step in not to arbitrate but to illuminate. Quick recommends this technique:

"First, the member asks permission to interpret each position for each side. The mediating member then asks whether that version reflects the disputant's argument. Such intervention can clarify the real differences and areas of agreement."

5. Harmonizing. Some debates get so heavy that the participants don't even realize that they actually agree on some points. The harmonizer analyzes their views to show how close they are to real accord. Next, he or she invites other teammates to join in.

6. Summarizing. Occasionally, an entire team can become so immersed in needless conflict that confusion takes over. At this point, a clear-minded team member comes forward and sums up the discussion. "This gives the group time to breathe, think, and restore confidence in itself and forces the team to look at how it is functioning — something that the group might not have done because it was too involved in details to see the whole picture," says Quick.

As an individual team member, you may find yourself in a position to play one or more of these various roles. If you do, be sure to step in and do your best. It will help your team move forward.

INFORMALITY INSPIRES TEAMWORK

In any work setting, most people perform best in an atmosphere of casual informality.

Neither professionalism nor productivity are compromised when team members are comfortable and safe. Rather, creating a relaxed backdrop to team interaction encourages the open exchange of ideas.

Glenn M. Parker, author of *Team Players and Teamwork* (Jossey-Bass), remarks: "One sign that your team is effective is that you enjoy being around the people. You *want* to come to team meetings. You look forward to the association and contact with your teammates."

In a strict environment that operates poorly, employees performed poorly there because they found meetings and social contacts so boring that they avoided them.

Says Parker: "A team with a positive climate bypasses such formal trappings as rigid voting rules and raising hands before speaking. An obvious ease of interaction and communication relaxes team members and enhances their contributions.

"Humor seems to be an integral part of successful teams. Members talk about team meetings as 'enjoyable' and 'fun' and even 'a lot of laughs.'"

If you look at the top teams in your organization, Parker says, you'll notice that formality is alien to their existence. People come to meetings early because they want to chat over a cup of coffee before the agenda begins.

The teammates look pleasant because they feel that way. They enjoy being there. And, when the meeting is over, many will stay longer to talk about team business or swap stories.

Parker maintains that informality can be encouraged by the time of day that team meetings are conducted. The ideal meeting times are early in the morning when people have time for coffee and conversation, just before noon so that the group can have lunch together, or at the end of the day when people may want to adjourn to a restaurant.

You also can help to create an informal team climate by:

• Providing necessary work resources without waiting for a formal request;

• Sharing the limelight with others after you've played a major role in an important team triumph;

• Helping teammates to get to know and feel comfortable with each other; and

• Using humor and discussion of nonwork topics as a way to relieve tension and smooth over awkward moments. However, avoid humor at the expense of teammates. It could backfire.

"Being part of an effective team is enjoyable," Parker observes. "When they're asked to report on their most pleasant work experiences, most people will mention a successful team, committee, or other group activity."

Mistaking Uniformity for Unity

"Synergy" is the habit of creative cooperation or teamwork. For those who have a win-win mentality and exercise empathy, differences in any relationship can produce synergy, where the whole is greater than the sum of its parts.

Synergy results from valuing differences by bringing different perspectives together in the spirit of mutual respect. Insecure people tend to make others over in their own image and surround themselves with people who think similarly. They mistake uniformity for unity, sameness for oneness. Real oneness means complementariness.

— Steven R. Covey, The Seven Habits of Highly Effective People (Personal Leadership Application Workbook) Covey Leadership Center

Communication Killers

When proposing an idea to teammates, beware of "killer phrases" that can stop your project cold.

Combat these killers with responses that put your proposal back on track:

- **"Get a committee to look into that."** A committee could sidetrack the development of your idea. Turn it into an advantage by being directly involved with the committee's actions.

- **"Don't rock the boat."** Illustrate the advantages of creating a change. Be specific in identifying the drawbacks of the status quo.

- **"We've tried that before."** It can be difficult to be open to an idea that has flopped in the past. But your advantage is that it happened *in the past*. Make it clear why you think the idea didn't work then and why it will work *now*.

- **"That will never work."** This statement is crushing in any context. Make it clear how it can work and what can be done to ensure the idea's success.

- **"It's not in the budget."** Suggest alternatives to keep the funding low — starting small for example.

- **"Yes, but ..."** Pay close attention to what follows the "but." Then immediately address that alleged drawback directly and try to change that "but" to a "yes."

- **"The boss will never go for it."** Revise the idea so that your teammates have more confidence in it. Try to look at the situation from your boss' view to find and solve possible problems before you present the idea.

FOUR WAYS TEAMS KEEP 'FIT'

Just as runners need training to win a race, teams need "fitness training" to secure winning results.

Fitness training teaches teams to cope with the problems caused by complex work situations, conflicting time demands, and limited resources, according to *Team Fitness* (ASQC Quality Press).

Meg Hartzler and Jane E. Henry, Ph.D., the book's authors, identify four principal areas of fitness concern and tell teams how they can meet their challenges:

1. Customer focus. This area exercises the team's awareness of customers' expectations, values, and priorities. The team members must be able to fashion their products or services to satisfy their customers.

"Customer focus is the heart of the fitness plan," the authors explain. "Everyone must understand the customer's needs and expectations so that every decision is made with an eye on the impact it may have on the customer." Remember to keep that heart pumping.

2. Direction. Teams tackle four critical factors to ensure they head in the right direction.

Their *charter* formally establishes the team. A *vision* creates a mental image of what the team wants to accomplish. The team *mission* defines its purpose, and *goals and objectives* spell out the desired end results and how to attain them.

"Direction is the mechanism that focuses actions purposely toward team goals," say Hartzler and Henry.

3. Understanding. Through understanding, teammates will learn how to capitalize on each member's strengths and differences. They will also gain a clear grasp of the dynamics of problem solving, decision making, and working within the organizational culture.

"Team members come to see each other as unique individuals and understand the strength that comes from diversity," the authors note. "They create a dynamic environment in which the resulting power and synergy help them to see a situation, opportunity, or problem from many different sides."

4. Accountability. In this process, the team agrees on how to reach its goals and how each team member will be responsible to each other and to their organization.

The elements of accountability include the *values and beliefs* by which the team lives, *operating agreements* that define work behavior, *project planning* to guarantee the completion of all work on time, and *implementation planning* to ensure that the team's work will be acceptable.

It should also be decided what, if any, corrective actions the team will take if a member does not live up to this individual accountability.

"Team fitness does not happen by chance," note Hartzler and Henry. "It requires concentrated attention to each of the four areas. All teams have areas of strength and areas that need focus. You might have to concentrate on one area for a time and then move on to another."

BEST MOTIVATION COMES FROM
TEAM MEMBERS

Everyone performs better when given reinforcement, and team members are no exception. But in a team situation, the most important feedback doesn't come from management.

"In a team environment, peer reinforcement is more important than boss reinforcement," said Ken Keller, partner in The Carroll-Keller Group, at *Inc.* magazine's recent Midwest Training Conference in Chicago. It is not traditionally a team member's job to provide feedback, Keller pointed out, whereas a boss is expected to give it.

When delivered correctly, peer reinforcement encourages repetition of the positives and prevents the negatives from recurring — thus creating an environment that will foster dedication to the team and its efforts.

The following are Keller's five characteristics of positive reinforcement:

1. Specific: When complimenting a team member on a job well done, be specific. "Hey, you're really great" will not produce the same effect as "Your suggestion to change the stations on the production line saved us $300 on the Phillips order. Great thinking!" As Keller points out, "A pat on the back does little to bring back behavior we want to see again."

2. Immediate: Any time lapse rapidly diminishes the value of positive reinforcement. Tell someone that you appreciate an idea immediately so that the situation and the suggestion are still fresh. Immediacy also will help you to be specific about the details of the action.

3. Achievable: Peer reinforcement should be delivered based on the individual's ability to achieve, not on a set standard. If a team member does something unusual or exceptional, that's the time to offer praise.

4. Intangible: Reinforcement should always be as intangible as possible to avoid conflict. Don't offer something material, such as taking a coworker out to lunch for helping you at work. Recognition through verbal praise is the best form of positive reinforcement. Material rewards raise coworkers' expectations.

"The more tangible the reinforcement," Keller said, "the more potential it has to create animosity among peers."

5. Unpredictable: Genuine reinforcement is usually spontaneous, since it is only delivered in response to a good idea or action. Scheduled compliments, such as praise at the close of each meeting, seem phony and often have the opposite effect they were intended to produce.

The hardest part of teamwork is maintaining a productive team. "It's far more difficult to keep a team going than to start a team," Keller said. "But if you practice peer reinforcement, you're one step closer to ensuring the continued success of your team."

QUICK TIPS

- **Ask, don't tell.** If you want a teammate's work to improve, resist the impulse to always explain how to do it. Instead, ask how the *team* can do better and how your teammate can contribute. This approach avoids confrontation and often sparks new ideas.

- **Suggestions welcome!** If your boss criticizes your team, seek suggestions on how he or she would have acted in the same situation, suggests Henry Rogers, author of *The One-Hat Solution* (St. Martin's Press).

- **Water Wizards.** Forget the old stereotype of the employee who wastes time at the water cooler, shooting the breeze with fellow employees. An MIT study shows that engineers who discuss work and share ideas are more productive than those who don't. Drink away!

- **Accentuate the positive.** Never say anything negative about yourself in the workplace. People tend to remember things you've done wrong, says consultant Thomas L. Quick. Don't give coworkers ammunition for thinking negatively about you.

- **Hear ye!** It's important that team members learn from each other's mistakes to reduce the odds of duplicating an error. So when a team member makes a mistake, it's OK to let everyone know about it ... but not in a condescending way. Take time out as a team to discuss what caused the mistake and devise methods to keep it from recurring.

Quiz

ADVICE ... WITHOUT OFFENSE

"Whenever someone on our team fouls up, it affects all of us. Our supervisor isn't always available, so another teammate might have to say something. What is the best way to do this without causing offense to a coworker?"

— J.P.R., Spokane, Washington

It is not unusual for teammates to find themselves giving work-related advice to coworkers. To find out if you are doing your best to give advice without giving offense, take the following quiz. Simply answer each question YES or NO.

	YES	NO
1. Do you avoid taking the lead when a problem arises in your area of expertise?	❐	❐
2. Do you try the indirect approach at first?	❐	❐
3. Do you speak quietly so others won't hear you?	❐	❐
4. Do you first ask the person what he or she wants or needs to know?	❐	❐
5. Do you refer to your own mistakes, in order to put the other person at ease?	❐	❐
6. Do you "speak with a smile?"	❐	❐
7. Do you wait for the best time to talk to the other person?	❐	❐
8. Do you avoid jumping to conclusions about the other person's abilities?	❐	❐
9. Are you clear and concise in giving your advice?	❐	❐
10. Do you periodically question the other person to make sure he or she understands you?	❐	❐
11. Are you diplomatic at all times?	❐	❐

Total Number of YES answers _____

ARE YOU A GOOD ADVISOR? Each YES answer is worth seven points. A score of 63 or above means that you are a diplomatic coworker. If you scored 49 or more, you are on the right track, but you should review the areas in which you answered no. If you scored below 49 you may need to work on your diplomatic skills before providing advice to a teammate.

PART II

SUCCESSFUL TEAM PLAYERS

CHAPTER 4

What Makes a Good Team Player?

"A team player isn't an isolated example, it's a way of life that is exhibited in everything they do — including others in decisions, pitching in ... looking for new ways of doing things."

— Kathy Zarr, Nothwestern Mutual Life

You are one link in a chain known as a "team." Here's how to be sure the links are secure and that you're pulling together with your teammates.

MAKING A NEW MEMBER FEEL WELCOME

Your team has inherited a new team member. You remember what it was like to be the new person on the team. What can you do to make her feel welcome?

Here's how you and your teammates can help a new member feel welcome and become productive in the team as quickly as possible.

• **Start slow.** You don't want to force a newcomer on the group. It takes time for both the group and the new person to be at ease with each other.

• **Provide frequent assurances.** An outsider is bound to feel alienated and alone. Provide personal assurances through conversations about work-related matters. Help this person gain confidence, which will make her more relaxed within the group.

• **Involve her in group discussions.** Try this approach: When discussing a problem with several other members of the group, say something like, "Let's see what Sondra thinks of this. She might have some good ideas." You want the others to begin feeling that the outsider is someone who may have a lot to offer.

• **"Quote" the newcomer.** Do this discreetly, as you don't want to appear to value her opinion more than you do the opinion of other team members. But on occasion you can pass along ideas and suggestions. This shows not only that you value them but that she has a valuable contribution to make.

• **Give it time.** Group dynamics change whenever a new person is introduced. It takes time for people to adjust. Don't push it. You don't want someone to feel left out, but a period of adjustment has a natural course to run. In time, she will be accepted as a "regular."

In Praise of 'Followership'

While great emphasis is placed on team leadership, don't forget the value of the roles of those who prefer to follow.

Robert Kelley, a professor at Carnegie Mellon University in Pittsburgh, says the flattening of organizational structures has increased the need for skilled followers.

As one example, Kelley tells of a large East Coast bank that was forced to reorganize and reduce its workforce.

The head of one department had recently trained his staff in self-management. In an effort to reduce the number of supervisors, he allowed them to operate without a leader.

Although skeptical, the bank's officers watched the team members grow in various follower roles. Each selected his or her own "followership" level.

Kelley places followers in five groups:

• *Sheep* are passive and uncritical. They perform assigned tasks and then await new orders.

• *Yes people* lack self-confidence and are lost without a leader.

• *Alienated followers* are independent thinkers who carry out their work roles with disinterest.

• *Survivors* play it safe. They adapt to change but seldom initiate it.

• *Effective followers* are typified by the bank's employees. They think for themselves, take risks, go at their tasks with energy, and can solve problems. In short, they're real team players.

WE ASKED: 'WHAT MAKES YOU A GOOD TEAM MEMBER?'

When was the last time you thought about the contribution you make to your team? We asked work team members what special skill they bring to their group. Here's what some of them had to say:

Pam: "I always try to say something positive when someone else in the group makes a suggestion. There is nothing worse than having all these people jump on you about having a 'dumb' idea. That's enough to make you never want to say anything ever again. There's something good about every idea, and I try to point that out first."

Juan: "I try to show up at all the meetings. In our company, it seems people get out of meetings a lot, and it's pretty much OK if you do. Well, a lot of times I could be doing something better, but I don't think you should treat the team like that. So even though it can be a hassle sometimes, I try to always go."

Mark: "I always make a contribution. I always pay attention and try to offer something. Sometimes I just feel like 'tuning out' a bit, or I'm tired of something, but I like to give the group my best effort. I wish other people would try that once in a while."

Odette: "I think the skill I bring to the team is that I am organized. I think our meetings would run wild if somebody like me weren't there to pull in the reins a little. This is a very creative group, and they don't pay attention to time limits or agendas. I know I come across like the school disciplinarian, but it helps get the job done on time!"

WHAT SIGNAL DO YOU SEND?

If you aren't being treated the way you'd like by other team members or your boss, you may be sending out nonverbal messages that say you aren't interested in your fellow workers or your job. Consider changing your behavior immediately if you:

• **Always arrive late or leave early.** Everyone has an occasional doctor appointment, sick child, or flat tire. But if irregular hours are a habit, you're telling people you don't care enough about your job to give it the time it deserves.

• **Ignore the dress code.** Individual style is admired to a degree, but clothing that shows disrespect for company heritage, decorum, or image can be resented.

• **Fail to help others.** You show that you are not a team player if you don't extend yourself to help coworkers on occasion.

• **Take frequent or long breaks.** Such behavior leaves the impression that you aren't pulling your weight in the office.

• **Turn in work that's sloppy or late.** Poor execution of specific jobs indicates that you cannot perform your tasks well or that you simply do not care to do the job right. Either way, you look careless.

'MY DOG TOOK THE CAR KEYS'
AND OTHER EXCUSES

Most team players know that chronic tardiness and frequent absences will cause projects to break down, deadlines to be missed, and morale to drop.

But it seems that a few employees still haven't gotten the message.

Accountemps, a major temporary-help supplier in Menlo Park, California, asked 150 executives from major American corporations to share some of the most unusual excuses they have heard for employee absences.

"Believe-it-or-not" responses included:

- "My dog carried away the car keys."
- "The wind was blowing against me."
- "I thought Monday was Sunday."
- "My favorite actress just got married. I needed time alone."
- "My best friend stole my car."
- "I felt it was better to sleep at home than at the office."
- "My husband's pet spider died, and I had to console him."
- "The engine on the yacht wouldn't start."
- "A plane landed on the highway and blocked all the cars."

Despite the humorous nature of this survey, its ramifications are serious. All your teammates should know that they are important to the success of the team. The team suffers in their absence.

OFFERING HELP FROM THE SIDELINES

Every competent work team solves problems, but you can go beyond that to share your teammates' difficulties.

"Wonderful ideas often are generated when people with different standpoints and approaches have a strong common interest in a certain job and come together for discussion," says Yoshio Kondo, a professor at Kyoto University in Japan.

Kondo, author of *Human Motivation* (Quality Resources), explains that this sharing experience is known as *okame hachimoku*, a term that means "the onlookers see better than the players."

The Pryor Report elaborates: "This phrase reminds us that people watching from the sidelines often have a more objective view than the players themselves."

When you have a problem, don't assume that asking for advice will slow team productivity. A teammate may notice something you've overlooked because you are too close to your work.

GOOD TEAM PLAYER — *NOT!*

Personal credibility is important in a team setting. When you have the trust and respect of your teammates, your ideas will be tested and your opinions will be heard.

But credibility is fragile, and you may damage it in small ways without realizing it.

Are you guilty of these credibility killers?

• **Promising things you don't deliver** causes teammates to mistrust your word. Be sure that you follow up on commitments and do what you say you will do.

• **Chronic tardiness** usually results in peers viewing you as unreliable. People generally aren't interested in hearing a wide variety of excuses. They just want you to be where you're supposed to be when you're supposed to be there.

• **Covering up mistakes** usually works only in the short term. Eventually, your teammates — and your supervisors — will discover the truth. You will be viewed as much more credible if you "come clean" when you have made a mistake and then do your best to fix it. Most mistakes are honest. Hiding them isn't.

• **Breaking confidences** is one of the most common ways people lose the respect of others. Eventually, teammates will be reluctant to tell you anything for fear of what you might do with the information. Ultimately, you end up being uninformed.

• **Criticizing or embarrassing others** does not make for solid team friendships. Public ridicule or making jokes at someone else's expense labels you as mean-spirited and insecure. If you have some legitimate feedback to offer someone, do it in private. Anything else is probably better left unsaid.

• **Refusing to consider other viewpoints** sends a message that you are inflexible. While there are times we must stick to our guns, often it serves us better to listen to others' perspectives and insights. Imagine the fate of your team if everyone refused to compromise!

• **Poor organizational skills** may seem like a minor offense, but if you constantly misplace things, forget appointments, and seem to have trouble managing your work, others will not have much professional respect for you. They may see your chaos as a reflection of your abilities — no matter how competent you are in other aspects.

You can't make your teammates respect you. You can only earn their respect through your words and actions.

Empowerment and You

If your employer has granted empowerment to your team, success will be measured by how seriously you take your responsibility.

Although each team shares the risks and rewards that come with empowerment, a work unit isn't a faceless entity. It's comprised of individuals like you who are aware of what personal contributions mean.

"To feel empowered is to feel a sense of control, a sense that you have the power to affect the work and the organization," observe Edward Betof and Frederic Harwood, co-authors of *Just Promoted!* (McGraw-Hill).

"Rather than feeling helpless, as on the dependent end of a parent-child relationship, employees who are empowered have a sense that they can exert control," the authors say.

Effective empowerment should engender in you these attitudes:

- You can improve the organization.

- Good ideas will be implemented.

- Even if your suggestions aren't accepted, they'll be appreciated and acknowledged.

- You and your teammates can be trusted with responsibility.

- You're respected for your ideas and judgment.

Betof and Harwood elaborate: "When managers remove barriers to effective performance and create a supportive climate, most employees will improve their performance. Some will achieve high levels of results."

Personal empowerment, the authors point out, should stir within you "a sense of commitment and alignment." You'll have the feeling that you and your teammates have an investment in the organization.

Moreover, you'll be convinced that you can effect its success. If you possess a sense of psychological ownership, you're certain to respond with a high level of responsibility.

All too often, however, the reverse occurs. Betof and Harwood tell of the mayor of a large American city who didn't believe in empowerment. He seldom consulted his aides, personally answered every question posed by the media, and made all important public announcements.

"He was seen as aloof and isolated, both from those who worked for him and those who supported him," the authors relate. "He increasingly viewed the job as *his* job, *his* city, and *his* responsibilities.

"As his top people sensed the erosion of their authority, their sense of ownership also eroded. Some left their jobs; others marked time.

"Responsibility for making things happen increasingly fell to the mayor, and he became less effective. He ended up with all the problems on his desk and no organization to manage them."

Empowerment is a gift to you and your teammates. Use it wisely. Recognize that individual involvement by each of you will lead to achievement for everyone.

WHAT TYPE OF TEAM MEMBER ARE YOU?

Most teams have four main kinds of members.

You can remember their names by thinking of "the four C's." They're the Contributor, Collaborator, Communicator, and Challenger.

In the next four articles, we'll take detailed looks at each of the four types as described by Glenn M. Parker in his book Team Players and Teamwork *(Jossey-Bass). From the descriptions, can you determine what type of team member you are?*

PART 1: CONTRIBUTORS 'WON'T LET THE TEAM DOWN'

"A contributor," Parker says, "is a task-oriented team member who enjoys providing the team with good technical information and data, does his or her homework, and pushes the team to set high performance standards and use resources wisely. Most people see the contributor as dependable."

As the contributor views it, team progress comes about through the sharing of expertise. He or she regards the team as a group of subject-matter experts whose function is to complete a series of task assignments.

"Contributors help the team by freely offering all the relevant knowledge, skills, and data they possess," Parker explains. "They realize they're on the team because they have certain information they're expected to contribute."

This attitude becomes particularly important when organizations turn to cross-functional teams to address customer problems and needs.

"At Digital Equipment Corporation, for example, such work groups provide customers with integrated solutions," says Parker. "Effective contributors are critical to the success of these teams."

In competitive environments, the author notes, some team members withhold information because they want to have an edge in performance appraisals. Such secretive behavior can destroy a team's entire purpose.

The honest contributor realizes that he or she was hired because of special skills. For that reason, contributors often make excellent team trainers. However, they sometimes become impatient with teammates who lack their fervor.

In some instances, contributors spend so much time helping teammates that their own tasks are left unfinished. When others must pick up where the contributor dropped the ball, well-meaning intentions instead engender team resentment.

Their discussions about work are filled with references to "quality," "excellence," and "results." Contributors' high standards and efficiency are reflected in their final reports.

"Reliable," Parker observes, "is often used to describe those whom the team turns to when quality and timeliness are important. The contributor does not let the team down."

Part 2: Collaborators are Goal-Directed

None of the "four C's" who make up a team is more goal-directed than the collaborator.

"The collaborator," says Parker, "sees the vision, goal, or current task as paramount in all interactions. He or she constantly reminds the team to stay on track and make sure that everything is focused on the target."

That target might be completing a new system or bringing a new product to market. Whatever must be done, the collaborator is always willing to pitch in.

Bill McClung, an executive at Johnson & Johnson Baby Products, views collaborators as "people who have the ability and willingness to do work outside their areas of expertise in order to benefit the team effort."

McClung cites a new-product team that loaded trucks all night to meet a test-market deadline. No one had "truck-loader" in his or her job description.

Collaborators are found at every level in teamwork-structured organizations. Parker points to a few managerial examples:

- A branch bank manager who opens a teller's window when the lines are long.

- A vice president of personnel who works into the early morning collating manuals for a training program the next day.

- A senior analyst who cancels a vacation because she learns about a system problem the night before she's scheduled to leave.

Says Parker: "Rather than just being good individual contributors, these team players derive satisfaction from being part of a successful team.

"They realize their contributions are necessary for success, but they don't require individual recognition to be satisfied."

As a result, collaborators see to it that their team has a clear mission. They help the team to establish both long-range and short-term objectives.

When the need arises, Parker says, collaborators become visionaries. Dissatisfied with teams that regard goals as little more than day-to-day "to-do" lists, they insist on goal-stretching exercises that extend over a period of time.

"The collaborator also brings the goal-setting process to the daily environment," Parker adds. "While the 'big picture' is important, the current task is also significant.

"Collaborative team players help the team to understand and clarify its immediate work assignment. They also realize that, without periodic reviews, the goal-setting process loses its credibility."

Even if it means changing team goals and plans, collaborators are always open to new ideas and data. And, because they have high levels of self-esteem, collaborators seek out critical feedback. They know that it will help them and the team.

PART 3: COMMUNICATORS KEEP THE TEAM TOGETHER

The communicator acts as the glue that binds the other three "C" personality types together.

Parker maintains that team contributors, collaborators, and challengers would have difficulty functioning as a unit without a solid communicator.

"We all know that the climate and culture of a team are critical to the success of the total effort," Parker says. "Climate influences such factors as productivity, creativity, and problem solving.

"The communicator contributes to a positive climate by helping people on the team to know and feel comfortable with each other."

As a process-oriented team member, the communicator performs several tasks:

- Resolves such team problems as conflict and lack of involvement.

- Listens carefully to all viewpoints but withholds personal judgment.

- Creates an informal atmosphere that helps the team relax and have fun.

- Recognizes and praises teammates for their efforts.

- Conveys enthusiasm and a feeling of urgency about the team's projects.

- Periodically summarizes where a team dispute is headed and calls for a consensus.

- Gently prods everyone to participate in discussions.

- Enables everyone to learn what skills and resources each member can contribute by encouraging team fellowship.

- Provides feedback to teammates that is descriptive, specific, and useful.

- Reminds everyone of the ongoing need to evaluate team effectiveness and devise plans to improve overall performance.

"The informal climate that is the hallmark of the effective team is facilitated by the communicator," Parker explains. "He or she initiates and supports pre- and post-meeting discussions of such nonwork topics as family, vacations, hobbies, and sports.

"Good-natured jokes and comments that break the tension or smooth over an awkward moment contribute to the team's effectiveness. The communicator uses humor, tact, and diplomacy to encourage informality and reduce destructive conflict."

Communicators, the author adds, are positive people who always see a glass as half-full rather than half-empty. As Jay Wright, an AT&T executive, puts it: "They have a 'can-do' attitude. These team players are energy givers rather than energy users."

In a recent survey Parker conducted, senior managers reported that "lack of recognition for performance" was their employees' main complaint. A communicator diminishes such feelings simply by saying, "Good job."

Communicators don't wear labels. But, if your team is performing as it should, someone — perhaps you — is striving to keep everyone together.

Part 4: Challengers encourage team
members to grow

The team challenger isn't out to win popularity contests. Indeed, by often going against consensus decisions, he or she soon learns that telling the truth can be costly — and effective.

Even so, the other three "C" team types — communicators, contributors, and collaborators — need a challenger to shake them up.

When this occurs, they may realize that there is a better way.

"Challengers are willing to 'swim against the tide,'" explains Parker. "They're candid, open, honest, and, above all, deeply concerned about the direction of the team.

"They very much want the team to succeed. However, challengers may appear to be a negative force because they express opposition to the prevailing thinking. The effective challenger opposes team direction with good intentions."

Parker cites these as typical challenger behaviors:

- Shares views about the team's work.
- When necessary, openly disagrees with the team's leader.
- Frequently raises questions about goals.
- Fights for high ethical team standards.
- Always speaks out, even when in the minority.
- Prods the team at meetings with tough "why?" and "how?" questions.
- By daring to differ with conventional wisdom, constantly faces the accusation: "You're not a team player!"

- Urges the team to undertake risks as long as they're well-conceived.

- Reports team progress and problems with total and often unwelcome honesty.

- Doesn't hesitate to "blow the whistle" if a teammate is engaged in unethical activities.

- Supports a legitimate team consensus when his or her views are rejected.

Says Parker: "If the corporate norm about teamwork is 'To get along, go along,' then the challenger won't be accepted as a team player. However, in that kind of culture, being accused of not being a team player is a sure sign of a courageous challenger."

Many team members, the author adds, dismiss the challenger as "the resident weirdo or cynic." But those who really care about the team's future regard the iconoclast as honest and authentic.

Challengers report team results accurately and expect their coworkers to do the same. They frankly assess their own contributions and urge everyone to talk openly about missed deadlines, quality problems, cost overruns, customer complaints, and dissatisfaction within the team.

"The mark of effective challengers is knowing when to stop pushing," Parker concludes. "If you're a real team player, you know when a consensus has emerged and it's time to move on. The challenger who doesn't know when to quit can be obstructive."

QUICK TIPS

- **Volunteer for team success.** Volunteering to help is essential to building teamwork. But be sure to volunteer for the right reasons. Will you be helping someone else or your team? Don't volunteer to "one-up" someone else; others will see through your intentions.

- **No time for wasting time.** Develop a mind-set that judges every activity in terms of whether it brings you closer, even minutely, to your goals. "Other people will tune in to your no-nonsense approach and learn to respect your time as much as you do," says Jeff Shalzman in *Careertracking* (Simon & Schuster).

- **Agreeing to disagree.** When you're making a critical observation, include some aspect that you *do* agree with. For example, "I like Sharon's idea that we try new approaches on this experiment. But because of our tight deadline and low budget, I don't think we can afford to change direction right now."

- **New members welcome!** How can you help a new member become a productive and welcome team member quickly? Try this: Provide frequent reassurances and make a point of involving him or her in group discussions. But take it slow. It's natural for your team to need some time to feel comfortable with a newcomer.

- **Problem people.** Experts say there are actually seven different ways team members approach problems: 1) Recognize a problem and solve it; 2) Rrecognize a problem and help others solve it; 3) Recognize a problem but don't know how to solve it and don't try; 4) Solve the portion of a problem that affects them personally; 5) Feel no responsibility for solving problems; 6) Recognize a problem, don't understand it, and quickly forget about it; 7) Recognize a problem but leave it to someone else to solve. The first and second approaches are used by effective team players. Are you effective?

ARE YOU OFF TO A GOOD START?

"I just celebrated my six-month anniversary on our team. Since I had never worked on a team before, I think it's a good time for me to review how well I've adapted to the concept of teamwork."

— K.O.R., Elmira, NY

Bravo! Your desire to review your progress is a good sign that you want to be a valuable team member. The following quiz can help you determine in other ways whether you're off to a good start. Answer each question YES or NO, then score yourself.

	YES	NO
1. Do you believe work teams improve communication?	☐	☐
2. Do you believe work teams increase productivity?	☐	☐
3. Has communication between you and your coworkers improved?	☐	☐
4. Do you enjoy the work you do?	☐	☐
5. Though you may not always agree with your team members, do you respect them overall?	☐	☐
6. Do you believe your team is making positive contributions to meeting the agenda of your company?	☐	☐
7. Do you strive for good relations with your fellow team members?	☐	☐
8. Has your motivation increased?	☐	☐
9. Has working with others helped broaden your perspective?	☐	☐
10. Has teamwork helped bring out the best in you?	☐	☐

Total number of YES answers _____

YOUR TEAM ADAPTABILITY RATING: Eight to 10 YES answers show that you have successfully accepted the new approaches you are encountering in teamwork; 5 to 7, and you are on your way. A lower score indicates you are fighting the concept. Learn more about the value of teamwork in your workplace.

CHAPTER 5

DYNAMIC TEAM DYNAMICS

"Coming together is a beginning; keeping together is progress; and working together is success."

— HENRY FORD

With the proper mix, the various personalities that make up your team all come together to create a powerful synergy. Here's the recipe to success.

NEW MEMBER CHANGES TEAM DYNAMICS —
FOR THE WORSE

Team dynamics have changed dramatically since Sara joined your group two months ago. She arrives late to meetings, sits in back, and seldom contributes to the group discussion. Team members are beginning to ignore her and are increasingly resentful. Productivity and morale have declined.

New members who join an existing team face great obstacles. The team already works comfortably together and may seem difficult to penetrate.

Sara is obviously shy. But even a more outgoing person can have a hard time breaking into a close-knit team.

Both the group leader and the team members need to go the extra mile to include Sara. In this instance, the team leader watched Sara closely and noticed when she seemed about to say something. Then the team leader intervened and asked her opinion.

To everyone's surprise, she spoke up with intelligent and useful suggestions.

Other team members took the cue and watched for opportunities to include Sara. In time she began exerting herself without coaxing. Sara is now an active and valuable team member because the team leader and the team worked together to recognize her potential.

WHAT LANGUAGE IS THAT TEAM SPEAKING, ANYWAY?

Small groups that work together daily, or even weekly, usually develop their own abbreviated language to discuss activities and facilitate decision making.

John F. Cragan and David W. Wright, authors of *Communication in Small Group Discussions* (West Publishing Co.), write about one group in which new members were advised "not to be a Greenwood." Though the new members were confused, veterans knew that Jack Greenwood was a former member who always used to come to meetings late.

"Over time," write the authors, "groups develop an elaborate array of idioms that are based upon the history of the group. It may take a new member several weeks or months to uncover the important incidents in a group's past that give meaning to the verbal expressions that punctuate the group's daily discussions."

Once that new member does understand the language, he or she will feel a sense of inclusion in the group and may enjoy watching the next new member looking on in puzzlement.

This "group-created language" is an indication of the relationships that team members develop. It reflects the way team members include each other and also the degree of goodwill that exists.

But minor problems can arise, say Cragan and Wright: "Sometimes group members mistakenly think everybody speaks their language and proceed to release public communiqués that contain the group's ideas encased in the group's jargon."

A team leader should be sure new members do not feel excluded. Other members should explain jargon to new members. And every team member should ensure the language is kept only within the group.

It can be fun to observe group language being exchanged. Sometime, stop and listen closely to what's being said. Your group's "language" is one quality that makes your team unique from all others. Listen closely and enjoy what you're hearing!

ETHICS AFFECT TEAM DYNAMICS — SOMETIMES SUBTLY

Suppose a teammate approached you one day and asked you to look the other way while he changed data on a team report to make the results look better. Could you do it? More important, *would* you do it?

Suppose your boss asks if you know why a close friend and teammate has taken so many sick days recently. Should you tell her that your friend has been interviewing with your company's competitors?

Or what if you're a team leader whose boss tells you to change the performance appraisal of a good teammate, which will compel this employee to quit, to save the company from paying unemployment?

We all face ethical dilemmas on the job, directly or indirectly. In today's competitive workplace, the distinction between shrewd and shady may be indiscernible. What may be unethical may not necessarily be illegal.

Whatever the case, ethics affect team dynamics. The effects can be subtle. Team members who suspect that another team member acts unethically, for example, may not be able to work with him or her successfully. Teamwork suffers.

If you're faced with an ethical dilemma, how do you decide what to do?

- **Summarize the situation.** Writing down the details can help you develop a clear perspective. List the sequence of events as objectively as you can.

- **Identify your concerns.** What's being asked of you? How do you feel about it? If you're having second thoughts about following through with an act, perhaps your conscience is telling you something.

- **Determine your options.** Then, list the anticipated outcomes for each one. Include a description of your feelings, teammates or supervisors who might be affected, and the risks you might face.

Going through this process demands complete candor with yourself. If you're still unsure about which route to take, consider these questions:

- Is your choice legal?

- Would you feel comfortable telling your parents, mate, or children about your activities?

- Would you feel comfortable reading about your actions on the front page of the local newspaper?

- Are you comfortable with what your decision says about you as a person?

Most of us have a sense of what is right and wrong, fair and unfair. Ultimately, we might "get away" with questionable behavior as far as others are concerned, but we still have to answer to ourselves.

DIVERSE TEAM TALENT BRINGS
OUT BEST IN TEAMS

Suzanne Willis Zoglio, Ph.D., an organizational psychologist, helps corporate clients manage change through planning, training, and team building. Through her management consulting firm, the Institute for Planning and Development, Zoglio has developed team-training programs for clients that include American Express, Bell of Pennsylvania, and Kellogg's.

Q. You've studied successful teams. What is the main characteristic?

A. Successful teams know where they are going. Everyone understands the team's purpose, goals, and mission. Too many teams shoot first, then draw a bull's eye around what they've hit. That's not motivating.

Q. What kind of goals should teams set?

A. Goals shouldn't be vague such as, "We will become the best service provider." Instead, goals should be something specific and measurable, so the team can judge how it's doing and recognize when it has attained a goal.

Q. What other ingredients go in the mix to make a successful team?

A. Diverse talent is important. Teams need some members who are strong in technical skills. But they also need self-leaders, people who can do what it takes without being told, and informal leaders who step forward and take charge when it's appropriate.

Diversity like this means some individuals may be well trained in technical areas but sorely unprepared to lead a group meeting. Other members might be quite proficient in group processes, but not in training. When there's a diverse balance of talent, a team can tap the wide range of ideas and talent present. It all helps booster the team's overall performance.

Q. Could such diversity also be a recipe for disaster?

A. Yes. That's why the next ingredient is so important: good team tactics. You can't just throw people into a room and expect them to work well together. Successful teams work on the process of being a team. No matter how much talent you have on that team, the group's going to fail if the team doesn't have a process worked out for solving team conflicts, building consensus, or handling team crises.

Q. If you could give a team one piece of advice, what would it be?

A. Don't sit back on your laurels. Stretch. There will be team changes and changes in your workplace, so learn to adapt. Think like the member of a team but don't miss any opportunities to grow personally.

10 TYPES OF TEAM MEMBERS

Ever since the 1940s when social scientists first studied work teams, they have been observing the various "roles" individual members play in their group.

Though the experts don't agree on exactly how many roles there are and how to name them, 10 general personality types have been identified:

1. Task leader. May or may not be the designated leader; a nuts and bolts, roll-up-the-sleeves-and-get-busy type.

2. Social-emotional leader. Concerned with the emotional heartbeat of the group; good at solving interpersonal problems.

3. Tension-releaser. "Breaks the ice" with appropriate humor at the right moment.

4. Information provider. Has research skills that stand out above all the others. Could end up doing unfair amount of the work.

5. **Central negative.** Always plays the devil's advocate role in discussions but in a nonthreatening manner.

6. **Questioner.** Constantly seeks clarification and more information.

7. **Silent observer.** Speaks little, observing and taking in all the information. When he or she does speak up, people listen.

8. **Active listener.** Listens attentively, sums up other points of view. Good at keeping discussion on track.

9. **Recorder.** Has good recording skills and little interest in participating in group discussion.

10. **Self-centered follower.** Constantly questions opinions in a nonsupportive way. Unlike the central-negative person, the self-centered follower is concerned mainly about personal interests.

A LITTLE PSYCHOLOGY CAN HELP

To interact successfully with others in your work group, it pays to know a little psychology. An understanding of the basic styles people use to communicate can help you understand members of your team better — and help you communicate more effectively.

Stuart M. Schmidt, a professor of human resources, and David Kipnis, a professor of psychology, have studied the different styles that exist within small work groups.

In one study, reported in *Psychology Today*, they broke down the six different types of strategies used by members of small work groups when they want to get their way: *reason* (writing a detailed plan); *assertiveness* (repeatedly remind); *friendliness* (make people feel important); *coalition* (obtain support of other team members); *higher authority* (appeal to the leader or other *higher authority*); *bargaining* (offer of help for what is wanted).

They then reported on four styles people use in work groups:

- **Shotguns.** People who refuse to take no for an answer.
- **Tacticians.** They rely on reason and logic to influence others.
- **Ingratiators.** They rely on flattery and "politicking" to get their way.
- **Bystanders.** They seldom try to influence others but instead stand by watching.

FIRECRACKERS OR STARS? WHAT'S YOUR *TEAM'S* PERSONALITY?

Just as individual personalities make up a work team, the work team — as a group — develops a personality of its own.

Management consultant Charles Aubrey has identified four common team personality types.

- **Party animals.** "They have great energy, but it is often misdirected into social activity with no obvious task orientation," Aubrey explains. Such teams need a strong leader to help keep on course.

- **Plodders.** "Extremely task oriented. They have to make sure there are no mistakes in their work so they check and double check."

- **Stars.** High achievers with a great deal of enthusiasm and direction. The danger is if management identifies them as the ideal group and neglects less visible teams.

- **Firecrackers.** Like stars, these teams have high energy and enthusiasm for their work. They differ from stars in that they do not hesitate to question authority. "Firecrackers want to get something done quickly to change or improve the organization, and their energy can be short-lived with erratic stops and starts," says Aubrey.

ROAD FROM 'STORMING' TO 'PERFORMING' CAN BE BUMPY

Has your team become so independent that it operates completely independently from your organization?

Too much team building focuses only on internal processes and fails to consider organizational missions, teamwork consultant Harlan R. Jessup asserts in *Training & Development*.

The first vital concept for teams is *sharing* — "sharing one mission, sharing tasks and experiences, and sharing consequences," says Jessup.

Together with bonding experiences that occur every day, team building is also one of a team's shared experiences.

The second vital concept is a team's growth process. Teamwork expert B.W. Tuckman has divided growth into four stages — "forming," "storming," "norming," and "performing."

When they're being formed, Tuckman explains, teams have high morale. As role competition develops, stormy days may lie ahead. Eventually, teammates return to normal and gear up for a high-performance effort.

However, the journey from storming to performing isn't always predictable and is seldom swift. Your team needs a road map. Jessup lists your principal companions and destinations on that journey:

• **Stakeholders, mission, and values.** "The basic objectives of any team," Jessup says, "are defined by a group of stakeholders. They include managers and customers, as well as teammates, support organizations, and special-interest groups that care about the team's product, processes, or results."

A team's mission, he notes, is simply a restatement of the expectations of prime stakeholders. It must accurately reflect the goals of the team and everyone who has a stake in the team.

Further, those expectations must create a set of values that drives your team to achieve its mission. They must be endorsed by everyone on the team and communicated frequently.

• **Vision, measurements, and structure.** The vision is your target. It indicates where you want to be at a certain time.

As you move along, Jessup elaborates, you'll need concrete methods by which to measure your progress. And, in a well-designed business structure, every team function becomes a building block. You must understand how team results contribute to overall business objectives.

• **Goals, action plans, and results.** "Goals represent incremental, short-term steps toward realizing a vision," Jessup continues.

And that vision needs to be expressed in very tangible terms. For example, rather than setting a goal of "improved customer service," state a specific measurement, such as a 95 percent on-time delivery rate.

Only once these goals are set can a team move on to a plan of action. "A set of viable goals may be viewed as a pivotal way station on the road from expectations to results," says Jessup.

As your road map leads you from one stop to the next, strive to attain continuous improvement that will enable you to consistently meet your stakeholders' expectations.

SUCCESSFUL TEAM MEMBER: WHAT'S YOUR SECRET?

What "secrets" do you use to work more successfully with others?

Margaret: "Sometimes I have a good idea and someone else will pick up on it and run with it. It used to bother me — I wanted credit for that idea! Now I enjoy it when the seed I planted is picked up by someone else that way. I let them think it is the greatest idea in the world and that they are great for coming up with it. Other people have done the same for me!"

Joanne: "I try to show my interest in what the other person is saying by asking questions. I really listen and dig below the surface, showing that I'm thinking about what they're saying."

Dale: "I like to try to be sure everyone's voice is heard in a meeting. I used to be very quiet and pretty shy. I was dying to open my mouth and say something. It always meant a lot when someone would say, 'What do you think, Dale?' Now I try to do that for others who may be hiding in the background."

Mark: "I take coworkers aside one-on-one and ask them their opinion of something I'm working on or considering. I've gotten a lot of valuable input that way, and I think people appreciate their opinion being sought."

Juan: "I try to repeat to people good things I've heard others say about them. It may be something I hear in passing and even fairly minor, but I think people deserve to hear good things that are being said about them. I know it makes my day when I get wind of praise, even if it's indirect."

10 QUESTIONS THAT KEEP TEAMS ON TRACK

"Is our team on track?"

That's a question every team should be asking itself periodically. The following 10 questions can serve as a starting point in a team self-evaluation.

For team members to maintain anonymity, the questions can be answered on paper and typed up together on a master sheet without attribution. Then, at a special team-development meeting, the collected answers can be discussed and corrective action taken. Here are the questions:

1. Do we trust each other?

2. Are we genuinely interested and concerned for each other?

3. Do we feel free to communicate openly?

4. Do we understand our team's goals?

5. Do we have a real commitment to these goals?

6. Do we make good use of all our abilities?

7. Do we handle conflict successfully?

8. Does everyone participate?

9. Do we respect our individual differences?

10. Do we enjoy being members of this team?

QUICK TIPS

- **Look for the overlooked.** Give more attention to the silent team-mate. It's too easy to fall into the trap of noticing only the loudest team member while ignoring the quiet ones.

- **Beat that rut.** When the team is in a creative rut, try this: Take a common object, such as a hair pin, door knob, or frying pan. Ask: "Does this object *have* to be this way? How could it be improved?" Tossing around ideas can reunite the team's creative spark.

- **Breaking silence.** To energize a quiet team member, ask concise questions and give the team member your full attention to show that your interest is genuine. Be concise and brief.

- **Small victories.** Recognize team accomplishments each week by having team members write down three good things that they helped "make happen." Then at the next team meeting, have each member read what they wrote.

- **Getting to know you.** Do the various teams in your organization know what each one does? To bring everyone up to date (and boost efficiency), conduct in-house seminars at which the teams explain their goals and activities to each other.

TIME OUT FOR A TEAM CHECKUP

"Our team seems to go from one project to the next. We never pause to evaluate how well we're doing as a team because everything seems to be going quite well. Is that approach OK?"

— T.P.K., SAN FRANSICO, CA

Though team members may be working well together, it's still important that your team pause occasionally to evaluate itself as a group. Team members should take this quiz individually, then discuss the answers. Even if all is well, the process of taking the quiz and sharing answers can help build a stronger, more unified team.

	YES	NO
1. Has your most recent team project reduced costs, improved a product, or helped improve time management?	❏	❏
2. Was the project completed on time?	❏	❏
3. Did your team leader explain the problem accurately?	❏	❏
4. Were all members involved in the problem-solving process?	❏	❏
5. Was everyone kept abreast of the status of the project?	❏	❏
6. Did the team seek management approval as needed?	❏	❏
7. Did the team keep management informed?	❏	❏
8. Does your team really value the concept of teamwork?	❏	❏
9. Has communication improved within the team as a result of this project?	❏	❏
10. Did communication improve between the team and management?	❏	❏

Total number of YES answers _____

YOUR TEAM EVALUATION: With fewer than seven YES answers, your team may want to spend more time on team-building techniques. See Chapter 3 of this book for suggestions.

CHAPTER 6

WORKING TOGETHER

"Teamwork is a plural process. It cannot be done by one person. When people come together to form groups, each member brings a personal set of knowledge, skills, values, and motivations. The whole is greater than the sum of its parts."

—ROBERT R. BLAKE, *SPECTACULAR TEAMWORK* (JOHN WILEY & SONS)

It takes patience, sweat, and a lot of effort to work together as a team. The good news: It's well worth the effort.

HOW TO TREAT DISABLED TEAMMATES

A disabled coworker has joined your team. She's going to be a valuable asset to your group, but you're concerned about how you should interact with her.

Above all else, remember to treat your disabled teammates as the capable, intelligent people they are. Author Mark Hequet offers some specific behavioral guidelines in *Training*:

- When talking to a teammate in a wheelchair, sit down.

- Don't give disabled people a condescending pat on the head or shoulder.

- Ask only once: "Is there anything you need?"

- Never use the word "handicapped."

- If you must use a translator to communicate with a hearing-impaired teammate, look directly at your peer, not at the translator.

- When you invite a blind person to sit down, gently place his or her hand on the back of the chair.

- If a disabled person offers to shake hands using a mechanical device, don't show any hesitation.

PERSUASION BUILDS TEAMWORK

Within your team, you must try to persuade the others that your ideas are sound. And, when you're dealing with management, skilled persuasion is even more essential.

"Fortunately, the art of persuasion is a learned skill," says Niki Scott, author of the syndicated *Working Woman* column. "What's also fortunate is that it can be learned at any age."

Here are Scott's tips:

- Know in advance precisely what you want from the person you wish to persuade. Be specific.

- Determine the amount of time, effort, and money that will be needed to grant your request.

- If what you want is going to be complex and time-consuming, say so at the outset.

- Research the advantages to the other person of cooperating with you.

- Be prepared to respond to any possible objections that may be raised.

- Keep your sales pitch brief. "There's a fine line between persuasion and harassment," says Scott.

- Always assume that your teammate's or supervisor's point of view is valid. You won't win by dismissing questions and objections out of hand.

- Be prepared to negotiate.

Finally, if you strike out, know when to quit gracefully. Many more work days lie ahead.

PROVIDING FEEDBACK — TACTFULLY

Two important parts of being a team player involve letting others know when their actions and ideas are good ones — and telling them tactfully and constructively when they're not, says Jim Lundy, author of *T.E.A.M.S.: Together Each Achieves More Success* (Dartnell).

The key is to direct your comments at the behavior exhibited or concept presented by your teammate rather than at the teammate directly.

"Focusing on behavior and actions, rather than traits, can make feedback more acceptable," says Lundy. "It leaves the recipient believing that change is possible."

If your feedback is critical, preface it with a positive statement: "I think you're on the right track with that cost-cutting proposal, and it could be even better if..." Notice that the word *and* is used rather than *but* to separate the compliment from the criticism. The word *but* often negates anything said after it.

'I RESOLVE ...' ISN'T JUST FOR THE NEW YEAR

Whether your team is newly formed or a fixture your company can't do without, its members should resolve to:

• **Support each other.** Of course, you can work as a team without feeling a sense of personal involvement. But why not get more out of the experience by letting yourself be genuinely concerned about your fellow workers? You'll get more satisfaction every day.

• **Take some chances.** Don't let your team grow complacent. Make the effort to find a new approach. Broadening your view and considering new ideas may help you reach the best solution.

• **Be patient.** We all have bad days when we simply don't perform well. Be patient when a team member is just not "clicking." You'll appreciate having breathing room yourself when you need it.

• **Accept each other's differences.** Diversity is what keeps your team on its toes. When you feel there are too many opinions in the air, sit back and take a deep breath. Smile and appreciate the differences that make each member — and the whole team —unique.

KNOW YOUR NEIGHBOR

Your team will become more effective when members learn about the other jobs and work teams within your company.

Bring your team together with employees from other departments so they can become acquainted and discuss their jobs. When employees discover the extent to which their work affects other departments, they are likely to become more responsible and quality-conscious.

YOU GOTTA HAVE TRUST

Your growth and advancement in any group are virtually impossible if you cannot win the trust of your teammates.

Here are some suggestions to help inspire their confidence:

• Show them that you're working for their best interest as well as your own. Peers want to know that your individual needs mesh with the team's.

• Share information to improve your organization. People may believe you're hoarding it to boost your ego.

• Admit weaknesses, concerns, and fears. If you are honest about these things, people will trust your sincerity in other matters.

• Show that you are well-informed and that you have considered coworkers' input in making decisions.

• Focus on issues rather than egos. Ask what will be accomplished for the business rather than who will be pleased.

• Don't let the grapevine beat you to telling teammates about bad news that affects them. Honesty is needed in bad times as well as good.

• Support employees' and colleagues' decisions. When they err, follow up immediately to help them learn from their mistakes.

• Admit your mistakes. People respect a person who admits he or she is human more than a proud one who must always be right.

'SET YOURSELF UP' FOR SUCCESS

Every team's success depends on an established set of criteria, says G. Michael Durst, Ph.D., president of Training Systems, Inc., in Evanston, Illinois.

Such criteria come from you and your teammates.

Durst refers to work units with top-ranking records as "PowerTeams." The members of such groups, he says, develop their own internal success criteria. Ask your team these questions when establishing criteria of your own:

• How will the team accomplish its task?

• Who will do what, and what standards must be met?

• What are the time limits?

• How will the team conduct itself with customers and clients?

PowerTeams, Durst adds, set themselves up for success by doing good groundwork. They must meet the success criteria and measure their achievements as they go along.

"This way," he notes, "members can continuously see where they're going and look back with satisfaction from where they came. There's a feeling of progress."

Pair up for Success

Aldina Fuentes was frustrated. Each month, as production coordinator for a financial printer headquartered in suburban Chicago, she was responsible for tracking scores of pamphlets and brochures. Lately, the accounting department kept changing its paperwork procedures weekly.

As a result, Fuentes often had to prepare a new report form, after being told that the one she had used last week was no longer acceptable. "Virtually nothing at work was routine anymore," she fretted.

Rather than grumble about the accounting department, Fuentes asked her boss if she and her coworkers could take advantage of a new company teamwork tool called pairing. In this organization, a "pairing" project is a way to bring together workers or departments, so they can come up with mutual solutions for any difficulties between them.

Fuentes related her frustration with the constant change in procedures. The accounting staff listened, then gave their reasons for the changes. As it turned out, the accounting department was shifting to a computerized financial tracking system and was testing various software programs. The result? Confusion.

The one-hour pairing meeting ended with an increased understanding on both sides. Accounting agreed to announce any changes as early as possible. Production has agreed to be more tolerant of the changes. They understood that the situation would be short-term and benefit the company's bottom line.

In short, pairing is a low-risk, low-cost way to enhance teamwork and efficiency within an organization. It doesn't require special equipment or a big budget. And it generally produces the kind of communication needed for any company to perform at its best. Here are pairing-project basics:

• **A facilitator.** This is usually another staff member, but one who has no connection with either party and no vested interest in the issue. The facilitator's job is to keep discussion moving and guide it in a positive direction.

• **Neutral territory.** A conference room, small auditorium, or even a small office can be suitable, as long as it provides a degree of privacy.

• **Positive attitudes.** Healthy skepticism is helpful, but participants should not enter into a pairing session predisposed to failure or personal victory. Pairings exist to inform and explain, as well as to search for solutions. Most times, misunderstandings or problems are not any single person's "fault." More often, problems are caused by flawed procedures or systems.

• **Follow-up, as needed.** In Fuentes's case, she invited accountants to take a tour of her work area. During that friendly, informal visit, she was able give them a better idea of her situation.

A pairing need not be so formalized or group-focused as the one above. Are you experiencing misunderstandings with a person in another department crucial to what your area does? Maybe a short pairing session with a neutral third party would help. You might be surprised how this information-sharing method can help you work better and build more productive work relationships.

'PIGs' HELP TEAMS WORK TOGETHER

If you're having difficulty working with the members of other teams, consider recruiting some "PIGs."

PIGs, "Positive Interdependency Groups," tie together team members' behavior and guarantee a winning result.

Too many organizations believe that pitting teams against each other will boost productivity, asserts Harry A. Olson, author of *The New Way to Compete* (Lexington Books).

Instead of motivating workers to do better, he maintains, contests among teams *demotivate* them. As they watch the same people from the same teams win all the prizes, a feeling of uselessness takes over.

Legend has it that a senior manager at General Motors walked into the factory one day, scribbled a number on the floor in chalk, and left with no explanation.

It took the workers only a short time to figure out that the number represented the automotive output of the previous shift. The chalk reminder became a daily ritual, and production accelerated as shifts tried to outdo each other.

Although the chalk stunt worked for a while, Olson says, it was a demoralizing tactic. Members of each shift began to view other workers as common enemies rather than fellow employees. Soon, teamwork deteriorated.

"Motivation in a team needs to be intrinsic, born from within the team itself," the author contends.

That's where Positive Interdependency Groups enter the picture. They create a healthy competitive environment where everyone wins and nobody loses.

Berol Chemical (Gothenburg, Sweden) organizes small project groups. Employees from production divisions work with research-and-development (R&D) personnel. Team leadership is rotated so that the R&D and factory employees have equal status.

To bring PIGs into your operation, try these four steps from Olson:

1. Rotate leadership. Berol Chemical illustrates how this can be accomplished. Equality promotes cooperation. When each teammate knows that a turn at leadership will come, team play functions at a peak level.

2. Ask for equal bonus sharing. This would have to be negotiated with your senior managers. To increase the likelihood of acceptance, make it clear that you want bonus pay divided equally and tied to team productivity gains.

3. Evaluate group performances. Team members would share the same evaluation at performance reviews. Again, this involves company policy. You can help to implement it by promising that your team will bring slow performers up to par.

4. Request cross training and job rotation. Few managers will argue with this concept. When everyone on the team has more than one skill, absences will have less effect on output.

By putting everyone in the same "pen," Olson says, a PIG team can outperform any other type of work unit. You'll be in the pink!

DIFFERENT TEMPERAMENTS AFFECT
TEAM DYNAMICS

Individual temperaments have much to do with how team members use their time, Merrill E. Douglass and Donna N. Douglass observe in *Time Management for Teams* (AMACOM).

"Teamwork is tricky," they remark. "We need individual skills to solve problems and meet team goals, but we don't want individuals to think of themselves as the center of the team. The secret to this everybody-wins situation is the knowledge and understanding of individual temperaments."

The authors identify four temperament types and their plus-and-minus characteristics:

• **Time taskmasters.** They're tops when it comes to leadership. They can guide your team to its goals. Time taskmasters are tightly focused and don't let problems get in their way. They take on risks and can bolster teammates who are timid. *However,* time taskmasters tend to be bossy and anger easily. They can be rude and insensitive. In addition, many are workaholics who make hasty decisions.

It's a question of balance. If they have positive attitudes, taskmasters are the kind of people that every successful team needs.

• **Time teasers.** Enthusiasm is essential for every team, and time teasers have it in abundance. They argue persuasively and create an environment in which the seeds of their ideas blossom and benefit everyone. *However,* time teasers like to talk endlessly. Because of their infatuation with conversation, they can waste their time and yours. And while they talk, they often overlook details and follow-up procedures.

• **Time terriers.** "These are the ultimate team players," Merrill and Donna Douglass contend. "Time terriers were born to be supportive, dependable, and faithful. They provide the stability, the cement, that holds the rest of the team together." *However:* "Time terriers can be worrisome and fearful, which, in turn, causes them to be stubborn and indecisive. They are usually not self-starters and tend to procrastinate. Frequently, the goal holds no attraction for them. This makes them indifferent to plans and resistant to change."

• **Time tenders.** Every team must have people who are absorbed with details. Time tenders furnish this valuable contribution. They think in a logical manner, ask questions that eliminate possible errors, and move one step at a time toward the team goal.

However, their preoccupation with detail causes time tenders to see negatives that aren't really there. They may proclaim: "It can't be done!" As perfectionists, they're hard to please. Moreover, they can become too introspective, moody, or even depressed.

"Each time-temperament personality can bring important skills to the team effort," the authors conclude. "Encourage each type to do his or her best. Positive relationships lead to positive results."

'EVERYBODY IS IMPORTANT!'

Championship football coaches remind us that everyone on a team is essential, Harvey Mackay points out in *Beware the Man Who Offers You His Shirt* (William Morrow).

When Ray Berry was head coach of the New England Patriots, he took Polaroid pictures of all the ball boys who assisted the team. Berry asked each to sign his name on his picture.

At a team meeting, the coach distributed the photos and instructed each player to learn the names that accompanied the faces.

"The boys know who you are," Berry told his team. "I want you to know them. Everybody's important."

And, when Notre Dame football coach Lou Holtz was at the University of Minnesota, he passed out T-shirts with *TEAM* printed in large block letters.

Barely visible below this was the word *me*.

DIVERSITY ENCOURAGES GROWTH

Team diversity is a fact of the '90s business world — and one that you should welcome.

If you don't think diversity in the United States will affect your team, these workplace statistics from *Voices of Diversity* (AMACOM) should change your mind:

- Women, people of color, and immigrants represent more than 50 percent of the present U.S. workforce.

- By the year 2000, 85 percent of the *entering* workforce will be female, African-American, Asian-American, Latino, or new immigrants.

- Within 25 years, one out of every four workers in the U.S. will be age 55 or older.

- Of the 43 million people with disabilities in the U.S., many will seek equal opportunity in employment, encouraged by the rules set by the Americans with Disabilities Act of 1990.

Teammates may be different from you in a number of ways, including age, religion, race, and physical situation. But they all have one thing in common — they will bring to your team a fresh set of ideas, perspectives, and work styles that will make your team more balanced and open to change.

A team in which all members agree, think alike, and hold the same beliefs is destined for stagnation.

From diversity comes change, and from change comes growth. All team members should constantly strive for the growth and development of the team.

HANDLING CULTURAL DIFFERENCES

As the American workforce becomes more diverse, effective teamwork requires everyone to learn how to deal with people from different cultures. Consultants Bob Abramms-Mezoff and Diane Johns, authors of *Success Strategies* (ODT Associates), outline three tactics to build such relationships:

- **Put yourself in the other's place.** Consider what it must be like to live in a new country, perhaps having a large family jammed into small quarters, or finding it difficult to express yourself in a language you don't know very well.

- **Be frank in uncertain situations.** Let's say that an Asian coworker avoids looking at you during conversations. In some Asian nations, direct eye contact is regarded as rude. If you can't clearly evaluate speech motives or behavior, just say: "I get uneasy when you don't look at me when we speak. Is there something wrong that I don't know about?"

- **Follow the Golden Rule.** Treat the other person as though that individual were actually you in disguise.

QUICK TIPS

- **Make it constructive.** Next time you criticize, make it constructive. Explain the task's purpose, its goal, and the specific steps taken. Criticism can work only if it provides a direction for improvement.

- **Understanding emotions.** "The best way to deal with others is to understand the power of their emotions," says author Roy Garn in his book, *The Magic Power of Emotional Appeal* (Prentice-Hall, Inc.). That will "help you get more job enjoyment, improve your persuasive power, and stimulate superiors to single you out for promotion."

- **In praise of praise.** Offering praise for a job well done is good for teamwork, but be specific. Instead of saying, "Nice job, Julia," say, "I really like the suggestions you made to increase computer use."

- **Shared deadlines.** If your team misses deadlines, the deadline-setter may take into account individual workloads and schedules. When the team is starting a project, announce that deadlines are set in stone. Then let team members set interim deadlines for meeting them.

- **Gifts for team members?** Etiquette does not call for exchanging gifts in the office, says Letitia Baldrige in *The Complete Guide to Executive Manners* (Rawson Associates). But if you get along well with team members, you may feel some uncertainty on the issue. Bring the matter up for a full discussion in the group. You may discover you aren't the only team member pondering it.

SHOULD I 'LOOSEN UP'?

"I conduct myself in a businesslike manner, since I know management is critical of employees who spend too much time socializing. However, my teammates seem uncomfortable around me. Should I loosen up and risk getting into trouble?"

—J.M., FRANKLIN PARK, IL

Good teams are often made up of people who truly like each other. So, being friendly to teammates in no way diminishes your productivity. In fact, it can improve it by contributing to a trusting team environment. Personal warmth is the key to forging team bonds. Do your teammates interpret your businesslike demeanor as being unfriendly? Take this quiz to find out.

		YES	NO
1.	Do you freely smile and greet teammates when you see them?	❏	❏
2.	Are you willing to poke fun at yourself?	❏	❏
3.	Do you socialize with teammates during lunch or break times?	❏	❏
4.	Do you disclose things about your personal life to show that you're human?	❏	❏
5.	Do you ask teammates about *their* interests?	❏	❏
6.	Do you sincerely compliment your peers?	❏	❏
7.	Are you aware that work and fun are not mutually exclusive?	❏	❏
8.	Do you realize that cultivating goodwill is critical to doing your job well?	❏	❏
9.	Do you share information with teammates?	❏	❏
10.	Do you share a sense of team play?	❏	❏

Total number of YES answers _____

YOUR CHILL FACTOR: A score of eight or more YES answers suggests that you connect well with your teammates. A lower score might indicate that your demeanor doesn't foster trust and caring from your colleagues. Don't mistake isolation for professionalism. Don't chill out—warm up!

CHAPTER 7

TEAM TROUBLE!

"Even a goat and an ox must keep in step if they are going to plough together."

— ERNEST DRAMAH BRAMAH

Every team runs into personality clashes and other troubles. But the successful teams find ways to overcome such obstacles.

THAT HURTS! A TEAM MEMBER DOESN'T LIKE YOU

A member of your work team dislikes you. You hear from others that he has made negative remarks about you. You've asked him if something is wrong but were told "everything is fine." You know better.

Simply take him literally about "nothing being wrong." That's the advice of management consultant and author Marilyn Moats Kennedy. She suggests saying to your fellow team member, "I'm really glad nothing is wrong, because if there were I'd like to try to do something about it. How about lunch?"

Kennedy says this puts your associate on the spot. If there's nothing wrong, as claimed, having lunch with you is the only polite thing to do. Begin increasing contact — join in at breaks and chat cheerfully before your work team meets.

Why this approach?

Kennedy says this forces your fellow team member to either warm up to you or to break down and admit that something is wrong. If he has made comments to other people, you owe it to yourself to improve the relationship or at least determine the problem. This assertive approach usually resolves it one way or the other.

TURN DOWN THE VOLUME!

Disagreements *will* surface in the workplace. But you can defuse the situation. Here are some suggestions from Dianna Booher, author of *The New Secretary* (Facts on File):

• **Try humor.** Change anger into laughter. Say: "And that concludes Round One!" or something else that might ease the tension.

- **Inject rationality.** Try to get both sides to express facts, not emotions. If subjective interpretations are left out, the two sides might even see they agree on some issues.

- **Seek common ground.** Remind everyone that they are on the same team seeking the same goals. This approach can provide a starting point.

"If all of these efforts in mediating conflicts between colleagues fail," Booher advises, "remember the adage, 'Live and let live.' Keep the parties separate until they've had time to cool off."

WHAT THEY DON'T KNOW MAY
HURT THE TEAM

Tension is running high because certain team members don't seem to respect the others. One smokes throughout the meetings; another is always late. What can be done about these difficult teammates?

Surprisingly, the problem may not be disrespect. It might simply be ignorance.

To help keep team members informed, the group should discuss its ground rules from time to time. *"Is smoking OK?"* *"What about bringing food to the meeting?"* *"Why is it important to be punctual?"* Questions like these should be discussed openly and a list of rules put together for the team, with the understanding that they have been agreed upon and should be followed.

An established team may take these rules for granted. But if, when a new member joins no one passes the rules along, hostility or anger may result when the rules are broken.

That's not fair to the new member. (Some teams prevent this by providing a list of ground rules in a "new team member kit.")

If a team has set and communicated ground rules, and members are violating them, the team should discuss changes. The team leader may say, for example, "We have not reviewed our meeting ground rules for several months now. I'd like us to discuss them to see if they need adjusting."

WORKING WITH A TEAM GROUCH

Is there a grouch on your team? If so, you know how difficult it can be to work with one.

Still, you do have to work together. *Practical Supervision* offers these ideas for dealing with an irritating teammate:

• *Don't overreact.* The grouch is looking for someone to irritate.

• *Don't play along.* Stay cool and detached.

• *Defuse the tension.* Use a little humor. Joking in a non-malicious way can lighten everyone's spirits.

• *Undo the damage.* Team leaders can assign temperamental workers tasks to do on their own so they aren't able to stir up the others.

• *Make expectations clear.* Try to find out what's wrong. The team leader should empathize if a personal problem is causing the behavior, but it should be clear that such moodiness must be kept out of the work group.

EIGHT *WRONG* IDEAS ABOUT TEAM CONFLICTS

Conflict can be a positive force in the workplace, but today's fast-paced business world can breed destructive conflict. More demands create more conflicts. Further, the situation seems to be worsening because of the numerous myths that surround conflict resolution.

These eight "wrong ideas" can prevent your team from building constructive conflict.

• **Wrong Idea No. 1:** "We can avoid conflict through effective communication and good management." Elaine Yarbrough, a conflict-management consultant to major corporations, claims that this is impossible. We must learn to live with and manage conflict, she says.

• **Wrong Idea No. 2:** "In a conflict, clearly state your position so that the other person knows where you stand." Because your position is probably obvious this often won't help much. What's important is that you actively *try to understand* your adversary's viewpoint.

• **Wrong Idea No. 3:** "Conflicts are always the source of blowups." As Yarbrough indicates, blowups are seldom related to the original conflict. They begin with a minor point that becomes overinflated and causes a misinterpretation of the disputants' true interests.

• **Wrong Idea No. 4:** "Encourage people to talk about the *real* issues causing the conflict." People's best interests are the issues that spark conflict. The problem is that many of us know our positions but not our true best interests.

• **Wrong Idea No. 5:** "You should deal with the conflict after people have had time to cool off." This strategy, Yarbrough maintains, is totally wrong. Delaying a resolution can give teammates more time to build up resentment toward one another. Tackle the conflict immediately.

• **Wrong Idea No. 6:** "If you're the person responsible for resolving the conflict, you must be controlled and have your act together." According to the consultant, you won't resolve a conflict unless you are concerned about it and are at least partially vulnerable.

• **Wrong Idea No. 7:** "Don't vary your style if you're the one responsible for the conflict. It confuses people." This leads to rigidity. If you're inflexible and don't know when to back off or move in, a mutually beneficial agreement cannot be reached.

• **Wrong Idea No. 8:** "You shouldn't do anything to increase the tension caused by a conflict." There are times when you must play for bigger stakes. For example, cite the consequences to your team if you fail to reach accord.

OOPS! DID I SAY THAT?

What can you do when you have said something you regret?

• **Apologize immediately.** If you wait, bad feelings can mushroom.

• **Don't fan the flames.** If an apology isn't enough, don't drag it on by continuously apologizing or bringing up the subject. Instead, make every effort to conduct yourself in such a way as to show that you didn't mean any harm.

Actions speak louder than words. Give it time.

• **Forgive yourself.** You can't turn back the clock and change what you've said. But you can learn from the experience. Teach yourself to take a breath before you speak when you're discussing a heated issue. And find a lesson in the experience: Learn to be more forgiving of others who commit the same error with you.

'Cooperative conflict' is
no contradiction

Successful teams don't have to avoid conflict — if they know how to manage it and use it to their advantage.

"The best possible world is where everyone is attempting to reach the best possible solution together, but where people feel free to challenge one another in the process," says Alfie Kohn, author of *The Case Against Competition* (Houghton Mifflin).

Here's how to create an environment of cooperative conflict:

• **Seek cooperation.** "Even if coworkers are friendly with each other, chances are they have not been in a situation that requires them to depend on — and be accountable for — each other," says Kohn. That feeling must be built by having everyone aim for the same goal, share the same resources, and receive the same awards.

• **Be sure team members feel safe.** "Everyone should understand that just because their ideas are being challenged does not mean that their authority or competence is being called into question," says Kohn. "No matter how heated a discussion may become, participants should always take care to avoid personal attacks." You're all in this together.

• **Aim for a consensus.** Modify decisions until each team member is satisfied. This encourages a productive discussion more than making a decision by vote. In addition, when all members feel that they have ownership of an idea, the support that idea receives is going to be much more universal.

"Remember that the point of expressing disagreement is not to put others down or promote oneself; it's to reach the best possible decision as a group," says Kohn.

Bank tackles team conflicts with 'Peer coaching'

For many years, Firstar Bank, a unit of Milwaukee-based Firstar Corporation, had been operating successfully by stressing customer service through self-managed teamwork. To combat new marketplace pressures, management decided to further improve customer service and use it as a competitive advantage.

The bank took a survey of the members of its 19 work teams in late 1993 to ask for ideas for improvement.

"Almost all the teams reported they needed help in two areas," says Linda Dewey, first vice president and division manager of the consumer division. "One was finding new ways to build trust among team members. The other was dealing positively with conflicts."

To address these concerns and thereby improve service, a process called "Peer Coaching for Individuals" was introduced by the bank's training and development manager, Maureen Gavahan.

The process, developed by Blessing/White, an individual and organizational improvement firm in Princeton, New Jersey, strives to improve one-on-one relationships between team members. Elements of relationships addressed include: communication with peers in other departments or functions; leverage of peers' skills, talents, and resources to meet individual and organizational goals; and the fostering of trust, teamwork, and peer support.

All members of self-managed teams at Firstar participated by developing plans for improving their relationships and increasing their individual contributions as well.

Once this program was completed, team members participated in another Blessing/White process, "Peer Coaching for Teams." Through it, participants define and clarify the team's focus and purpose; identify and access necessary resources; build commitment to the team and its goals; and develop successful action plans.

"We explained to participants that managing conflict is a positive process," Gavahan says. And, doing so without involving a manager is what self-managed teams are about, she adds.

These team-coaching sessions yielded positive results, according to Dewey. "Establishing house rules was particularly effective," she says.

"Teams were able to focus on what's important," agrees Gavahan. "They developed action plans for improving their effectiveness. Team members are meeting on an ongoing basis and continuing to improve."

CAN'T SAY THEY DIDN'T TRY

A Japanese company tried an experiment in which its employees were put in a padded room and given clubs, reports *Careers* magazine. The idea was that they would vent their anger on the walls instead of one another and this would result in calmer, healthier employees.

Instead, the experiment resulted in making employees more prone to violent behavior and within six months the room was dismantled and the employees' clubs taken away.

OUR DAILY DEALINGS

How much difference do we make to the people around us? Doesn't how successful they are really matter more to them than anything we could say?

Actually, our daily interactions affect family members' and coworkers' happiness far more than we might think.

An argument, rejection, or a put-down can put us in the dumps. A pat on the back, an award, or a new opportunity increases our happiness for a while. But the effect usually lasts for just a day or two. Then our moods return to normal, with ups and downs reflecting the next day's events.

The size of our paychecks and the importance of our titles matter little a few days after we receive them. It's our daily dealings with other people that affect well-being most. We build each other up, and we tear each other down every day. So, ponder what kind of difference you've made to someone else today.

— PAUL FRIEDMAN

EDITOR, *THE PRYOR REPORT*

WATCH OUT FOR PERILOUS TEAM PERSONALITIES!

Learning to work with coworkers is part of being a conscientious member of a team.

Sure, you can choose to deal with "challenging" personalities in ego-satisfying ways, such as giving a piece of your mind or ignoring anyone who bothers you. But such approaches usually cause more problems. A side effect is that you inadvertently increase your own stress. No one is worth that price.

Here are healthy methods for dealing with three trouble-some personalities, recommended by Juliet Nierenberg and Irene S. Ross, authors of *Women and the Art of Negotiating* (Simon & Schuster):

- **The spoiler.** This type finds fault with everything. His or her focus is typically on problems, but never on solutions. Most likely, he or she is sour and critical of coworkers.

To deal with this personality effectively, document all agreed-upon points with witnesses. On a project, watch how you phrase ideas. Spoilers look for the loophole. Best defense: optimism.

- **The pressure cooker.** This person is typically aggressive, loses his or her temper, and likes getting the upper hand, even if it means embarrassing others.

It's tough to keep cool in the face of a pressure cooker. When he or she loses control, excuse yourself until the situation cools down. When confrontations are mild, maintain eye contact and a firm stance. Remember that the pressure cooker explodes to gain or maintain control. Listen; don't argue. Best defense: Deal unemotionally with the facts.

- **The bulldozer.** This person is a coward in disguise. He or she seeks out the weak spots in others, takes on a superior attitude, and never admits wrongdoing.

Keep close wraps on your own weaknesses. When psychological pressure is applied (to either give in or assume blame), hold your own. Be clear about your objectives and maintain a calm, interested position. Best defense: Friendly, logical resistance.

With all three of these negative team players, remember: you *can* control your reactions.

DON'T GET 'LOST IN THE SHUFFLE'

The very nature of teamwork can make members fear losing their identity. But that doesn't have to be the case.

The individuality of the 1980s has given way to flattened corporate hierarchies and team situations in which once-traditional roles have become reversed, notes *Chicago Tribune* writer Cynthia Hanson.

As a consequence, highly complex job relationships have emerged. People must simultaneously fit in as team players yet hang on to their piece of the turf.

"Teams aren't necessarily an American phenomenon," Lynda McDermott observes in *Caught in the Middle: How to Survive and Thrive in Today's Management Squeeze* (Prentice Hall). "We come out of an individualistic cowboy-cowgirl culture."

Teamwork doesn't have to counter that. It doesn't demand that we think and act like cogs in a workplace wheel. The best teams are composed of people who sharpen their skills, go after difficult assignments, and challenge those who encroach on their rights.

Mickey Kinder, a teamwork and leadership consultant in Indianapolis, advocates "supportive confrontation" within teams. If your boss assigns one of your project ideas to others, address the issue.

Says Kinder: "People need to have their names on their contributions. You should tell your boss, in private, why it's important for you to be involved in those projects and the consequences to your morale and productivity if you're not."

If you feel that the team isn't using your talents, say so. "You might say, 'I've been a team player, but I'm getting lost in the shuffle. I want us to work on this together,'" notes McDermott.

As supervisors and managers suddenly find themselves members of work groups that they once controlled, even more bitter turf wars are likely to develop.

"Role clarification is vital," says Melanie Mills, a Denver consultant who conducts team-building seminars. Employees may have to remind their former bosses that the structure of their work relationship has changed, she says.

Two fundamental turf-protection tactics can help you maintain your individuality.

First, select your confrontations with care. Because you'll seldom agree with all your teammates, enter into only those battles that are worth the effort.

"Before you go to the mat with a teammate over turf," Hanson says, "ask yourself whether his or her behavior is a pattern that, ultimately, will impede your long-term agenda. If so, it's smart to speak about the problem before it escalates further."

Second, always speak and act professionally.

"You should be able to tell the truth in a healthy manner," Mills advises. "For example: 'My intention isn't to fight you. But I want us to understand my role and your role so that our jobs don't overlap.'"

WATCH FOR HIDDEN AGENDAS

Sometimes an undercurrent of tension in a work group has no obvious source. If so, hidden agendas may be at work. A hidden agenda results from prejudice, personality conflicts, or leadership aspirations members carry with them.

Hidden agendas are not always easy to spot, but there are several steps to take to help the group work out its hidden agendas:

- **Watch for them.** Don't pretend hidden agendas don't exist. They may lie under the surface, but everyone at one time or another reacts out of a prejudice.

- **Acknowledge them openly.** One way to bring them to the surface is to say something like, "I wonder if we have all said what we feel about this matter? Why don't we take some more time to see if there are any more thoughts?" A little more discussion time may be all that is needed.

- **Don't embarrass anyone.** Don't chide people about their hidden agendas ("All I'm hearing is someone grinding an ax"). Communication in the group will come to a halt if people are singled out that way.

- **Keep judgment out of the discussion.** Is the atmosphere in your team one in which members feel they can say what's on their minds without being judged? If so, hidden agendas are more likely to surface and be worked out for the benefit of the team.

RIGHT AND WRONG WAYS TO
MANAGE CONFLICT

When properly managed, conflict can promote creativity, lead to better decisions, and initiate beneficial change within your team structure. Conflict is managed — although not always successfully — in varying ways:

- **"My way ... or the highway."** This is a "win-lose" strategy. The winner proves he or she has more power than the other — and can force the loser to accept any solution. But a forced decision can lead to team sabotage or underground resistance. At best, a forced solution gains no enthusiasm or commitment to the principles of the winning side.

- **"We're one big happy family."** Smoothing over conflicts may involve securing a mutual "kiss and make up" strategy — for the good of the team or organization. But if this strategy does little to resolve the real causes of the conflict, it seldom leads to an effective, long-term solution.

- **"I don't want to talk about it."** Withdrawal or avoidance is wise when tempers get so hot that reason evaporates. But conflicts must be addressed at some time, and this takes a cool head.

- **"Let's compromise."** A well-designed compromise benefits all parties and reduces hostility. But it doesn't guarantee that future conflicts will not develop. A compromise works only if teammates trust one another.

The best solutions involve addressing and discussing with your teammates the actual causes of the problems. Effective resolution produces no losers and reduces the chances for future conflict. Here are some guidelines to manage conflict effectively:

- **Directly confront the opposing party.** Sidestepping issues or merely alluding to them only adds fuel to the fire.

- **Examine biases**. Before addressing a conflict, put aside personal prejudices. Then, you can keep these biases from interfering with issues.

- **Get personal feelings up front**. Often, issue-oriented conflicts are heightened because of personality problems. This often-overlooked variable can remain long after an issue is resolved and become the basis for new conflict.

- **Minimize status differences.** Agree on a neutral site for discussion, such as a meeting room. Using status or seniority as leverage in team conflicts leads to coercive compliance, not resolution.

- **Eliminate blame.** Fixing blame serves no useful purpose and only breeds defensiveness.

- **Don't hold out too long.** Rigidity can be a stumbling block. Smart communicators know when to push harder to gain more ground — and when to be flexible.

- **Identify mutual agreement.** No doubt, you and your teammates agree on something. For example, you have to agree that a conflict exists to take steps to resolve it. If you agree on the causes, you can develop workable solutions.

WATCH OUT FOR TEAM SABOTAGE!

Is your team under attack from destructive behaviors? Try these defenses, suggests teamwork trainer Steve Bucholz in *Creating the High-Performance Team* (John Wiley & Sons):

- **Judging.** This behavior occurs any time a teammate's ideas are discounted as "wrong." Request information to better understand ideas: "I see it this way. How do you see it?" suggests Bucholz.

- **Superiority.** This attitude comes when team members cite rank or seniority to suggest their views are more valid. Instead, strive for equality: "Our different viewpoints give us a better chance of covering every angle."

- **Certainty.** In this case, team members imply that they know all the answers and don't need any help, says Bucholz. Ask them: "What do you see as the key issue here?"

Quick Tips

- **When to argue ...** Every battle isn't worth fighting. Avoid arguing when the problem is only temporary and when you can answer "no" to the question, "Is this really important enough to argue over?"

- **... And how to argue.** When you must argue: 1) Try to see the other point of view first. Understanding how your teammate arrived at his or her point of view can help you clarify yours; 2) Don't get personal. You'll only be tuned out; and 3) Stick to the issues at hand. Don't bring up old frustrations.

- **Up in smoke.** Though fewer workplaces allow smoking these days, your team may at times meet outdoors or in a public place where smoking is OK. What should you do if the smoke is a problem? Bring the issue up to the team as a whole. Like every other team matter, discuss it freely without judging other team members.

- **Find the need.** When no one is agreeing on a solution to a problem, change the approach. Instead of looking for a solution, get a consensus of what *need* must be met. "Other options may then be discovered that can satisfy all the parties involved," says Robert Bolton of Ridge Consultants in New York.

MANAGING CONFLICT TO IGNITE CREATIVITY

"We're in an industry where creativity and the team conflict that accompanies it are essential. I try to manage my idea people tactfully, but I often wonder how well I'm doing."

— H.H.L., RENO, NV

The test that follows is based on one that the editors at Crisp Publications wrote for *Rate Yourself as a Manager*. Use the scale below to rate yourself after each statement.

MILD AGREEMENT							STRONG AGREEMENT		
1	2	3	4	5	6	7	8	9	10

Rating

1. When I'm buying team supplies, I'm not bothered by asking for a lower price. ____

2. If I'm reasonable, I have nothing to lose in seeking a better deal. ____

3. Conflict is a fact, and I work to resolve it. ____

4. Because it makes me examine my ideas, conflict is positive. ____

5. As I try to resolve a conflict, I consider my teammates' needs. ____

6. Conflict often produces the best solutions. ____

7. Conflict stimulates my thinking and sharpens my judgment. ____

8. Conflict has shown me that compromise is not a sign of weakness. ____

9. When satisfactorily resolved, conflict can strengthen relationships. ____

10. Conflict is a good way to test your own point of view. ____

Total Score ____

YOUR CONFLICT RESOLUTION SKILLS: If you score 80 or above, Crisp's editors say, you understand negotiation and have a realistic attitude toward conflict and its resolution. Between 50 and 79, you need a more positive approach. A lower score indicates that you must work hard to master the techniques of conflict resolution.

PART III

TIPS FOR
TEAM LEADERS

CHAPTER 8

MOTIVATING THE TROOPS

*"Thousands of geniuses live and die every year undiscovered —
either by themselves or by others."*

— MARK TWAIN

**Tapping the talent and resources of their team members makes
the most effective team leaders stand out.**

MOTIVATIONAL AWARDS

Your CEO has asked each team to appoint a member to serve on a special company-awards committee. She wants "something new" in employee motivation. You are your team's delegate.

Try these ideas suggested by William Finnie in the *St. Louis Business Journal:*

• Avoid such terms as *prize* and *competition*. They translate into *winners* and turn all the other team members into *losers*.

• Do away with individual awards by getting teams to outperform themselves.

• Make motivation a year-round tradition by announcing results monthly. More frequent recognition will ensure steady cooperation.

• Have more than one awards dinner a year. Present plaques, rings, or other enduring reminders of success.

BOOST MORALE WITH TEAM NEWSLETTER

If you're looking for a way to boost team spirit and share important information, publish a work-team newsletter.

Many teams publish newsletters along with the minutes of their meeting. The newsletter can also be distributed to management and other work groups.

What would a newsletter include?

For starters, develop a logo and a name. (The name can simply be the name of your work team.)

Include articles about the team's progress in solving problems or news of other group activities and the impact your team's work has had on the organization. You may also want to include information about unique approaches or ideas that have emerged in your team or other teams.

Don't forget to have fun with the newsletter: Include cartoons, a calendar of social events, birthdays of team members, interesting experiences, or motivational quotes.

FIVE WAYS TO REFUEL TEAM MOTIVATION

Your team is doing "OK," but you know it could be "outstanding." What can you do?

Pennsylvania-based organizational consultant Suzanne Zoglio says that a key ingredient to invigorating a team is to set goals.

There are techniques that can help. Zoglio, who is the author of *Teams at Work* (Tower Hill Press), offers these five tips:

1. Encourage risk taking. No one feels motivated when new ideas aren't cultivated and encouraged. "Let team members know it's OK to stick their necks out," says Zoglio. "Create a climate where the team has no reason to fear creativity."

2. Praise team members who take risks. Team members will maintain a high level of motivation when they've had positive reinforcement in the past.

"When someone offers a far-out idea, praise the person for their original thinking," says Zoglio. "When someone takes an unpopular position, praise their courage to 'swim upstream.' When team members risk looking foolish by asking questions, praise their willingness to clarify a point for the team."

3. Keep quiet! Some team leaders do so much talking, team members don't have an opportunity to open up. This stifles their motivation. One technique Zoglio recommends is to hand out three paper clips to each team member. When you speak, take one of your paper clips away. Then don't speak again until every other team member has spoken and turned in one paper clip. That helps ensure that everyone will make a contribution before you speak again.

4. Show results. "How did your team's last great idea positively impact the organization? How much money was saved? How many customers gained? How many accidents prevented?" When you show team members the impact their contributions make on "the whole picture," you inspire team members to greater heights of creativity and innovation, says Zoglio.

5. Accent the W.I.I.F.M. Team members will feel more motivated when they realize the impact their actions, as a team, have on the organization. But you can really get their juices flowing by helping them see the impact their contributions make on *themselves*.

Zoglio calls this the W.I.I.F.M. (What's in it for me?) factor. Ask team members what they've personally experienced from contributing in the past.

"Their responses will be personal and varied," she says. "For some team members, the reward is in knowing that they have had the opportunity to utilize their talents. For others, the reward is in being liked and appreciated by fellow team members, or just experiencing the satisfaction that comes from having learned something new."

But once they see the benefit for themselves personally, they'll be quick to make a contribution — and continue doing so for the life of the team.

SOME MOTIVATIONAL IDEAS WORK ...

• **Story time.** At Kaset International, a service quality consulting and training company, teams meet once a week to discuss different professional and development books. One member summarizes one to three chapters of the current book, and a discussion follows about how the principles can be applied to their team.

• **Where'd they go?** You never know where you'll find the quality-control team at Leckers, an Ohio manufacturing company. The team leader surprises members by holding regular meetings in a different location each week. "We've been in the production plant, the research lab, and even outside on the front lawn," reports a team member.

... AND SOME DON'T

• **What? No pumps?** When the male members of a Chicago-based telemarketing team fail to meet their sales quota, they must wear a woman's dress for a full work shift. "It's motivation by humiliation," says one disgruntled staff member.

• **Write up THIS dumb idea.** At a Western utilities company, a team leader publishes "The Dumb Idea of the Month." "He thinks it's funny, but it's just embarrassing," says a former team member.

What really motivates?
The $1 million question

While researching team motivation, business trainer Mark Sanborn was surprised to learn that less than 10 percent of the team members he spoke with had been asked one basic question.

"Without knowing the answer to this question, you'll never be able to effectively motivate team members," he says. "That's why I call this the $1 million question of motivation."

The question: "What motivates you?"

"The only way to motivate team members," Sanborn says in his book *TeamBuilt* (Master Media Books), is by observing and asking questions "to find out what hits their hot buttons and motivates them."

Here are some other questions you might ask your team members:

- What do you like most about your job?
- What do you like least?
- When do you feel you do your best work?
- Who do you work best with?

"Answers to these questions help team leaders identify the diversity of values, wants, and desires within a team, and provide the information necessary to tailor motivation to individual team members," says Sanborn. This approach then helps team leaders align members' personal motivations with those of the team and the company.

'CREATIVE COMMUNICATION' WILL GET THE JUICES FLOWING

Does your team need a motivation boost?

Just call Barbara Glanz.

The author, speaker, and consultant is practically *bursting* with ideas for "getting the creative juices flowing" in the workplace. Based in Western Springs, Illinois, she's compiled 399 real-life how-to examples in her book *The Creative Communication* (Irwin Professional Publishing).

Glanz spoke with us about her ideas:

Q: How does "creative communication" improve motivation?

A: Creative communication adds spirit to the workplace. For far too long most business communication has been predictable — and boring! I try to show people how to rise above the dullness.

Q: How about an example?

A: At Hydro-Electric, one of Scotland's electric utilities, employees are invited to "indulge in some healthy, satisfying bureaucracy bashing!" Every employee can nominate a policy, practice, or procedure that gets in the way of extraordinary customer service.

This type of communication differentiates that company from others and builds positive interaction. And Commercebank in Coral Gables, Florida, has the "Dazzle" program. A department chooses a person to be "Motivator of the Week." This person wears a hat for easy identification and is responsible for "pumping people up" when they run down.

Q: Your book says your goal is to "whack" a reader's thinking. What do you mean?

A: In his book called *A Whack on the Side of the Head*

(Warner Books), Roger von Oech says we are all bound up in "mental locks." We need something to "whack" our thinking, to help us see in a new way.

One of my goals is to whack readers into finding creative ways to communicate, to get the creative juices flowing. I am frequently asked: "How can we get our team motivated?" My answer: Be creative in different ways that surprise, even stun.

Q: Have you whacked someone lately?

A: Of course! When I speak before a group, I line the walls with 50 or 60 flip charts filled with inspirational and thought-provoking quotes. People love them because they regenerate the spirit and get them thinking in different ways. It's a great way to start a meeting.

Q: What makes team members *lose* their motivation?

A: In all the talk about quality, downsizing, and technology, we've forgotten the human being. Creative communication brings it back where it belongs — to one-to-one communication that treats people with respect as unique, living, breathing human beings.

MOTIVATED OR MAULED?

"There are two kinds of motivation," says Kurt Hanks, author of *Motivating People* (Crisp Publications): "motivation that's needed, and the kind that isn't."

Unwanted motivation occurs when teams that are already doing well are pushed to do *really well*. "Nothing is more frustrating than to have somebody try to gear you up to do what you've already been doing," says Hanks.

Are you guilty? Such team leaders, says Hanks, create a new program and a new approach. "That's where the mauling begins. Where things were going so well before, suddenly there are problems."

EVEN SUPERSTARS NEED SUPPORT

Helen Keller once observed: "The world is moved not only by the mighty shoves of the heroes, but also by the aggregate of the tiny pushes of each honest worker."

Each of your teammates is a uniquely gifted *individual*. When personal job skills are integrated into one finely tuned workplace machine, winning teamwork results.

"The sensitive team leader will help to create an open environment in which associates are empowered to reach out creatively to expand and improve the scope and quality of the individual contributions of the group's superstars," James L. Lundy points out in *T.E.A.M.S.: Together Each Achieves More Success* (Dartnell).

"In essence, he or she will facilitate opportunities for people to achieve and be recognized. At the same time the fully effective leader will maintain a communicative, coordinated, and cooperative environment to foster group, as well as individual, success."

Powerful companies often begin as entrepreneurial start-ups fashioned through the vision of one man or woman. But, as they grow to maturity, individual innovation gives way to group efforts and skilled leadership at every level.

Lundy cites one compelling example: "It was the genius of Chester Carlson that led to the invention of xerography, but it was a team of engineers and scientists who brought it to practical status and an additional team of thousands who helped people acquire and use the equipment."

General George Patton had such a dominating presence that some branded him as a poor team player. But he knew how to foster teamwork.

Fifty years ago, he said: "You know why I'm a great leader? Because I tell my men *what to do*, but I never tell them how to do it."

Says Lundy: "Peak-performance teams learn to accommodate the needs and interest of all types of teammates.

"However, as good team players themselves," says Lundy, leaders must "welcome feedback and be responsive."

Recognize the contributions of your superstars. But remember the words of Samuel Johnson: "No degree of knowledge attainable by man is able to place him above the need for assistance."

KEEP TEAM MOTIVATION ON TRACK

Over a period of time, work teams that are not monitoring themselves are likely to begin losing their motivation, explains Ralph Barra in *Putting Quality Circles to Work* (McGraw-Hill). He points out some early "storm warnings" that team members and leaders should be concerned about.

1. *Watch for*: Arguments that take the place of team discussions and simple voting that replaces seeking a consensus. (A consensus is not voting — it's the logical result of productive discussion.)

What to do: The team leader should address the problem in a special meeting. "Review the idea of consensus and emphasize a win-win situation versus a win-lose situation," suggests Barra. "The consequence of a win-lose situation occurring frequently is team failure, and the team leader must make sure that everyone is aware of that."

2. *Watch for*: Members who no longer participate. When this occurs, subgroups, or cliques, can form, and they can disrupt the goals of the whole team.

What to do: In most groups, other team members will force such apathy into the open for discussion. But sometimes the team leader must intervene. "The person or persons causing the problem must be confronted so the reasons can surface and a solution can be worked out," says Barra. "If the person or persons continue to be uncooperative and are unwilling to accept the role of a member, they should be asked to leave the team."

3. *Watch for:* Team detours from a predetermined process. Early on, a team establishes processes for the members to work within. A sure sign that the group is deteriorating is when members ignore such processes. Though it's natural for a group to enjoy a degree of flexibility, team members should be alert to wandering too far off track.

What to do: Usually, a gentle reminder from a team member or the leader will suffice if the problem is observed early on. Also, practical meeting agendas and minutes help keep the group focused.

WATCH OUT FOR THESE ROADBLOCKS!

Teamwork can spell success both for individuals and for work teams. But some members accustomed to working alone fail to see the benefits of working as a team. Watch for these roadblocks:

• **"I work better alone."** In *Psychology Today*, Roger and David Johnson, two of the leading researchers on cooperative learning, say such thinking is common because as children the emphasis in school has always been on individual achievement rather than on working with others. "Teachers keep kids separate and quiet," explains Roger Johnson, "yet research on how kids best learn goes the opposite direction."

• **"I have to stand out to succeed."** These individuals worry that their individual contribution will not be recognized in a team. Srully Blotnick, a business psychologist, has found this to be the chief concern of 6,000 workers he interviewed about teamwork. The solution: "Always try to put your personal stamp on each important project. You'll emerge a recognized expert."

- **"Teamwork is nice but it doesn't really work."** In *Spectacular Teamwork* (John Wiley & Sons), Robert Blake says this thinking is common in people who have been on unsuccessful teams. They need to be on an effective team where "seeing is believing."

This training is for the dogs!

Lloyd Gilbertson encourages team leaders to treat their teammates like dogs.

Well, sort of.

Owner of Caribou Creek Sled Dog School in Chatham, Michigan, Gilbertson teaches people to work with and race sled dogs as management training.

"You never ask a dog team to do something they're not prepared for," he says. "The same goes for your employees."

To train his clients to be better leaders, Gilbertson takes them, in groups of six to eight, on a cabin retreat. During the five- or six-day trip, group members learn to manage and care for sled dogs, working toward a race on the second-to-last day.

Gaining insight into management and leadership skills is the theme. Among those skills are decision making, adaptation, communication, and teamwork. Each skill is developed through interaction with the dogs, learning to work with their unique personalities, selecting the dogs for each team, and, finally, leading the dogs in the race.

"The barriers break down because everyone's starting from the same place," Gilbertson says. "You can't just assign a leader because some people may be better at some jobs than others."

The trips emphasize skills essential for team leaders, especially the people skills.

"In this information age, between the paperwork, taxes, and technology, people can get so busy that they lose track of people skills," he says. "The trips help them realign their thinking and give them a more effective way to manage."

HELP GET YOUR TEAM UNSTUCK

You bring an innovative new proposal to the table. You feel that spark, that invigorating feeling that comes when a winning new idea is about to take flight.

Then the team begins offering feedback:

"Gee, I don't know. We'll never get anyone else to agree to this."

"When management gets a look at it they'll change everything anyhow."

"This won't fly. Let's just forget it."

You feel like the wind has been knocked from your sails. You're ready to sink back in your seat, defeated.

But don't give up!

This team is stuck, and the challenge of the team leader is to get them unstuck.

So says Steve Buchholz, Ph.D., senior vice president of Learning Systems and Services at Wilson Learning Corporation. In his book *Creating the High-Performance Team* (John Wiley & Sons), Buchholz shows how to break the barrier built by apathy and get your team back on the road to high productivity.

The main reason teams get stuck, Buchholz says, is that they believe previous experiences dictate what they can and cannot do in the future.

"A common initial reaction to change is resistance," says

Buchholz. "Past experience has taught that 'It won't matter anyway'."

Buchholz says the most important way to overcome this learned apathy is to recognize it for what it is, describe it, and challenge the team to find creative ways around it. Here's how:

1. Recognize. To recognize learned apathy, listen in group discussions for phrases like: "This is the way we've always done it," "We're not going to change their minds," "We don't have the authority to enforce it."

2. Describe. Once you've recognized learned apathy, describe to the group what is occurring. Do so as objectively as possible to avoid defensiveness. For example, "I hear what you are saying. Based on our past experience with attempting to computerize the budget, it seems unlikely it will work."

After acknowledging the potential negative outcome, go on to describe a potential positive outcome: "But if we could get the budget computerized, it would save hundreds of hours and would eliminate human errors."

3. Challenge. Once the group is aware of what they have said and you have described the consequences, challenge them. "Ask them to give you ideas on how to make the proposal work or implementing whatever is required for change," suggests Buchholz.

Helping a team recognize and deal with their own learned apathy is a key to getting a group unstuck, he says. The result is a team that looks forward to growth and change.

LEADERSHIP: SCHWARZKOPF STYLE

Nowhere is teamwork more critical than in the military. When national survival is at stake, men and women may be called upon to make the ultimate sacrifice. Leadership can be the difference between life and death, victory and defeat. And nobody embodies it to a higher degree than U.S. General H. Norman Schwarzkopf.

In a *Personal Selling Power* magazine profile of the Gulf War hero, Gerhard Gschwandtner observes: "General Schwarzkopf commands attention, respect, loyalty, dedication to duty, adherence to a plan, and, most important, the love of the people who serve under him. Without that, no leader can make people perform to maximum capability."

The author cites four Schwarzkopf qualities that are as important in the workplace as on the battlefield: the ability to make decisions; a determination to set and stick to goals; self-discipline; and the power to communicate.

The French magazine *L'Expansion* notes that Schwarzkopf's Gulf War style included one other element that has a startling parallel in the world of work. The general treated his troops as if they were *customers.*

Gschwandtner explains: "He knew that in order for them to execute his commands, he had to deliver the proper equipment and supplies — on time — to the right place, not just one time, but every time."

A video titled *Take Charge!* (The Washington Speakers Bureau) zeroes in on the secrets of Norman Schwarzkopf's success. His leadership principles:

• **Help people succeed.** "People go to work to succeed, not to fail," the general reminds us. It's a leader's duty and responsibility to guide associates to success.

• **Don't confuse management with leadership.** If your manager can't provide it, you must look within your team for leadership. When people aren't led properly, they can't work well.

• **Set goals everyone can understand.** During the Gulf War, the goal of the multinational forces in Saudi Arabia was stated simply: "Kick Saddam Hussein out of Kuwait!" They did.

• **Establish high standards.** Work groups, Schwarzkopf stresses, must set high standards for themselves. "People want to know what's expected of them," he says, "and we all want to know how we're going to be measured."

• **Make room for improvement.** As one probably apocryphal story goes, Saddam once asked his staff to suggest how Iraq could end its war with Iran. One officer outlined a plan.

Saddam supposedly took him outside, shot him, and asked the others: "Does anyone else want to share a good idea?" The lesson: He saw no real need for change and eventually suffered the consequences.

• **Take charge!** Schwarzkopf says: "There's nothing more debilitating than to have everyone quivering with anticipation while nobody acts."

• **Do what's right.** "When the time comes to take action," he advises, "you'll have to do what's right. You'll know that you've done your best when people respect you."

QUICK TIPS

- **'Idea breakfasts.'** Informal monthly breakfasts with your teammates are ideal times to solicit improvement ideas. Schedule the meals so they coincide with a teammate's birthday or other special event.

- **Real motivation.** When you interview a prospective new teammate, ask these questions: "What's the most rewarding work day you've had this year? Why?" The answers give you insights into which activities and achievements *really* motivate a team member.

- **Quick boost.** Give swift recognition to a teammate who corrects an error or skills deficiency, says Don Bagin of *Communication Briefings*.

- **Fresh-air refresher.** When you're having a bad day, give yourself and your team a breather by going outside. Even if only for a few minutes, deep breathing and a change of scene can help restore the mind and body.

- **No-cost motivation.** Peter B. Stark, a consultant in San Diego, suggests these no-cost motivation techniques: Always shake hands with any team member who has done an outstanding job. Send a teammate to a meeting in your place. Tell your teammates how much they were missed after an absence and give an example of how.

CAN YOU MOTIVATE YOURSELF?

"I have just been assigned to a new team. I am sure that I can handle my new responsibilities as soon as I get used to them, but for some reason I am finding it difficult to get motivated. Can you help me understand why?"

— T.M.L., Los Angeles, CA

When people find value in their work, they also find motivation by meeting goals they have set for themselves and by meeting the objectives that their supervisors set for them, says Thomas L. Quick, author of *Successful Team Building* (AMACOM). The following quiz, adapted from that book, may help you understand what you can do to motivate yourself. Simply place a true or false after each statement.

	TRUE	FALSE
1. I work primarily for the satisfaction of doing my job well.	❑	❑
2. I look to myself for motivation rather than to my supervisor.	❑	❑
3. I welcome suggestions for improvement because they make my work better.	❑	❑
4. I set goals for myself when I tackle new assignments and strive to meet those goals.	❑	❑
5. I try to find ways to enjoy what I do, even when it's routine.	❑	❑
6. I share my desire to do my job well with my supervisor.	❑	❑
7. I reward myself when I meet my goals, rather than wait for the approval of others.	❑	❑
8. When my work is criticized, I remember not to take it as criticism of me as a person.	❑	❑
9. I try to see how my work will help me meet my long-term as well as my short-term goals.	❑	❑
10. I try to remember that every failure is an opportunity for growth, especially when trying to master new tasks.	❑	❑

HOW SELF-MOTIVATED ARE YOU? If you marked any of the above statements FALSE, you already recognize areas in which you need to change to increase your motivation or your new team. Start tackling those areas one at a time, so that you can be a more productive member of your team.

CHAPTER 9

ENERGIZE YOUR MEETINGS

"It's easy to get good players. Gettin' 'em to play together —
that's the hard part."

— CASEY STENGEL

Try these time-tested ways to get more from your team
at every meeting.

MAKING THAT FIRST MEETING A SUCCESS

A new work team has been formed in your department and you've been named to lead the first meeting. What can you do to make it a success?

The first meeting of a team can be the most difficult because members need time to adjust to the situation and to feel comfortable. But the first meeting is also crucial. Important business takes place. In addition, the whole tone of the group is set in that first hour the team spends together.

What follows are key activities that should be scheduled for that first meeting. Including them can help get the team off to a good, organized start:

1. Make introductions. Team members introduce themselves, discuss their particular job, and explain any expertise they may have. In addition, they might take a few minutes to discuss some personal information, such as their outside interests or hobbies. Such a free exchange helps to put everyone at ease and facilitates work relationships.

2. Choose a team name. An enjoyable activity, choosing a name allows team members to relax and to share ideas together. Usually, it will break down the tension that exists between people meeting for the first time, and it will often bring out creative and humorous suggestions. In addition, it begins building bonds among team members and formally identifies the team as a group.

3. Elect a team leader and a secretary. The team votes on a team leader (if one hasn't been appointed in advance). Votes are taken for a secretary, who will keep minutes, distribute marketing agendas, and do any other paperwork.

4. Distribute working kit and supplies. Some companies do not provide any supplies. Others provide kits with pens or pencils, loose-leaf paper, transparencies, notebooks, folders, and, depending on the project, sometimes even a carrying case.

5. Review goals and objectives. Often a member of management joins the team for this segment to explain what the team should be shooting for and to give management support.

BEATING MONDAY MEETING BLAHS

Are your Monday morning meetings anything but lively? Here are six ways to shake things up:

1. Ask open-ended questions.

2. Call on team members directly.

3. Ask people to come prepared.

4. Use silence and wait for answers.

5. Share personal examples; encourage others to do so as well.

6. Hold them on Tuesday.

MUSICAL CHAIR MEETINGS

Want greater participation in your team meetings?

Try mixing everyone up.

Most people are creatures of habit, taking the same seats at every meeting. Some peers may even arrive early to secure the "power seat" next to or directly across from the team leader, from where they can establish eye contact and monopolize discussion by holding the meeting leader's attention.

Before your next meeting, you can discourage this practice by labeling conference room chairs with the names of team members to be in attendance. Assign people to places they don't normally sit.

This new arrangement can serve to shake things up. For example, putting a shy teammate at the end of the meeting table, where people's eyes are naturally drawn, can encourage him or her to contribute more to the discussion.

10 TIPS FOR MEETING SUCCESS

1. Start — and end — meetings on time.

2. Facilitate discussion — don't preside.

3. Share the agenda.

4. Keep information for everyone to see on a flip chart.

5. Be sure someone is keeping minutes.

6. Don't let the process become bogged down.

7. Set goals of what you'd like to see accomplished for each meeting.

8. At the conclusion, summarize the results of the meeting.

9. Repeat commitments, deadlines, and follow-up duties.

10. Encourage everyone to participate.

SOURCE OF MOST PROBLEMS?
LACK OF PLANNING

Many people chosen to lead workplace meetings assume that their biggest problem will be one-to-one clashes.

But a five-year research program at 10 multinational corporations reveals that such outbreaks seldom occur. Only 3 percent of those surveyed cite personal disputes as a significant cause of meeting disruption, Carol M. Barnum reports in *Communication Briefings*.

"The remaining responses from 1,000 managers and technical professionals," she notes, "focused on meeting organization and lack of planning and preparation."

Barnum says that you must concentrate on three elements as you organize a team meeting:

• **Planning.** Never call a meeting until you've determined its purpose and activities. For instance if team changes are the topic, a "commitment chart" might be helpful.

"Draw up the chart by listing the key players who will be invited and their positions on the issue," she suggests. "Also, list your plan for winning to your side those people whose commitment is critical."

• **Notification.** Professional meeting planners consistently give this advice to group leaders: "Never conduct a meeting without an agenda."

Advance notification should include the date, time, and location of the meeting; a brief description of the items that will be covered; how much time will be devoted to each subject; and instructions for pre-meeting preparation.

• **A meeting action plan.** "Before you start the meeting, assign one person to use a meeting action plan," Barnum says. "Devise a form to record notes about actions taken during the meeting, the people responsible, and completion deadlines. Having someone else do this frees the team leader to lead the meeting and gives you a summary.

The seating arrangement can also be important. For example, there should be no "head of the table" in a brainstorming group because everyone has equal status.

But a decision-making session gives the leader an opportunity to lead. In that setting, you'll be most effective in a location designated for a chairperson.

HOW TO RUN A PRODUCTIVE MEETING (REALLY!)

Does anyone like team meetings?

Few team members would place meetings high on their "I-enjoy" lists, but they're essential And good meetings can bolster your chances for success in any project.

"It's difficult to have productive meetings because few people know the rules and skills needed," says Peter R. Scholtes, author of *The Team Handbook* (Joiner).

"In fact, the goal of having constantly improved meetings may be as hard for the team to reach as the improvement goals set for the project. Even so, you can learn new ways to work together by following guidelines."

Here are Scholtes' meeting basics:

• **Use agendas.** The current one should have been drafted at the previous team session and later developed in detail by you and a teammate. Send it in advance to all participants.

An agenda should briefly cover every topic to be discussed. List the names of presenters; time allotted; and a special notation if necessary — for example: "Must make decision."

Go over the agenda at the last minute to add new items or delete unneeded ones. If the session is to run for as long as two hours, plan a midway break.

• **Name a facilitator.** This person's task is to keep the meeting focused and moving. Leaders often serve as meeting facilitators, but you may want to rotate the role among teammates.

The facilitator's other principal responsibilities are to intervene if discussion breaks up into multiple conversations; prevent anyone from either dominating or being overlooked; and know when to end the meeting.

- **Take minutes.** Says Scholtes: "Each meeting should also have a scribe who records key subjects and main points raised; decisions made and assignments given; and items that the group has agreed to discuss again later. Rotate this duty among your teammates."

- **Evaluate the meeting.** Take the time. Get feedback on how to improve next time and begin a new agenda.

- **Stick to the "100-mile rule."** If you were meeting 100 miles from your workplace, it's unlikely that anyone would be called out to take a phone call. Unless it's a real emergency, enforce the "100-mile rule." Everyone stays put until the meeting is adjourned.

MAKING ORDER OUT OF CHAOS

If your meetings get out of hand, consider following *Robert's Rules of Order,* which is regarded as the authority on parliamentary procedure.

The rules spell out guidelines for conducting an orderly meeting, from determining whether a quorum is present to calling for adjournment. Among others, it includes rules for proposing a motion, debating, taking a vote, adopting a budget, and keeping minutes.

Most small work groups might not need such a structure, but adopting some of the rules can be useful for any meeting.

SEATING ARRANGEMENT CAN
IMPACT MEETINGS

Thinking back on your last team meeting, did everyone contribute to the discussion? If not, the seating arrangement may have been to blame.

The placement of tables and chairs at a meeting can have a profound effect on the outcome of the event. Here are a few alternatives for seating:

• **Theater-style.** Typically, in this type of arrangement, chairs are placed in straight rows with either one or two aisles. This type of seating is best suited for presentations delivered to large groups. It limits group participation, since participants don't face each other, and the focal point is at the front of the room. A warmer modification is to arrange the chairs in a "V." This allows the speaker to get closer to more audience members.

• **Classroom-style**. This arrangement is the same as theater-style, but with tables added. It is often used in training situations in which the trainer is the focal point. Placing the tables in a "V" shape builds more intimacy and encourages more interaction.

• **"U" shape or horseshoe.** Tables and chairs are placed in a "U," or horseshoe, with an open end. This formation creates a power position at the open end. The "U" shape is good for training and audiovisual presentations, and promotes more dialogue than a classroom arrangement, since participants can see each other. One drawback: If the "U" is squared off, people sitting in the corners are somewhat invisible and may feel left out. Round off the corners.

• **Hollow-square.** This is a closed square or rectangle, or tables and chairs with an open space in the middle. If you want everyone to participate equally, this arrangement works well because there is no position of power. However, it is not well-suited for audiovisual presentations because no matter where you place a screen or monitor, someone's back is to it.

• **Boardroom-style No. 1.** Also known as a conference-style arrangement, 10 to 15 participants sit around an oblong, boardroom-type table. This type of seating arrangement sends a message that the meeting is serious and that participation is important. It is not well-suited to audiovisuals, though, since some people will have their backs to the screen. Some seating positions are stronger than others.

• **Boardroom-style No. 2.** Using a round table for a meeting of up to 10 people sets up an intimate arrangement that encourages people to interact.

As was the intention of King Arthur in Camelot, there are no powerful seating positions. This arrangement serves as an equalizer.

When it comes time for your next team meeting, you must decide on the level of intimacy you want, as well as the amount of interaction you desire. If possible, you're smart to tailor your seating arrangement to suit your meeting's particular goals.

BEATING MEETING DEADLOCK

Meetings can get deadlocked, and the wise team leader knows what approach to use to break the silence. Consultant James H. Shonk recommends a technique called "snapshot."

In *Effective Meetings Through Teamwork* (Shonk & Associates), the author says, "Go around the room and ask each person to take no more than 30 seconds to respond to a question such as: "What do you think the problem is?" "What did you get out of the last discussion?"

Getting team members to react quickly can bring new ideas out in the open that otherwise would have never been considered. And that can end deadlock quickly.

'THE LAST GOOD MEETING I ATTENDED . . .'

Ed, Advertising Account Executive: "The last good meeting I attended was when our ad team was about a month old. We had gotten over the initial 'shy' period, where no one said much, and now we were really flying. Everyone was enthusiastic and the level of energy was fantastic. I wish we could have kept everything at that level, but now everyone seems to be settled into routine."

Melvin, a medical student: "The last good meeting I attended was, unfortunately, not a meeting I was participating in. Our class was sitting in on a meeting of a team of neurologists at our hospital. They were discussing a patient that one of the doctors had trouble diagnosing. It was fascinating to watch them go back and forth with ideas. There seemed to be no egos involved — they were really looking for a solution and not trying to outdo each other. I came away really respecting them and their work."

Diane, Personnel Administrator: "The last good meeting I attended? I can't think of a meeting that was very good!"

Terri, a mom: "This sounds crazy but the best meeting I ever attended involved my son's Scout troop. They were meeting to discuss their canned-food drive. They were so organized and so serious, and they were all prepared with an agenda and a list of assignments for each other. It was like watching a meeting of little adults, except these children were much more tolerant and respectful than most of the adults I know."

BRING THIS MEETING UNDER CONTROL!

Whether or not you are the team leader, you have a say in seeing that the team meets its goals for each session. If conversation strays from the topic at hand, sessions run late, or the meetings have turned into social hours, you should take action.

Suggest to the group that future meetings allot specific amounts of time to each agenda item. For example, a discussion of new assignments may be scheduled for 10 minutes of the meeting. Then, when you see a session running late, you can help get it on course by referring to the time schedule.

Another way to stay on time is to schedule specific business appointments to follow the meeting. Then you can legitimately excuse yourself when the designated completion time arrives, especially if conversation has drifted away from business issues.

One team member solved the problem by organizing a weekly luncheon of team members after the meeting. At the lunch, they could freely do all the socializing they wanted without infringing on regular team meeting time.

ARE WE ON COURSE?

Here's a simple test to help marketing leaders determine whether they keep their meetings on course:

Try doing a short memo summarizing briefly the actions of a particular meeting before you hold the meeting. In other words, do the minutes of the meeting before it takes place.

Do these minutes by first establishing in your mind your goals and objectives. Define the actions taken in terms of your definition of success.

Then comes the moment of truth: After the meeting takes place, compare your minutes with what actually happened.

When Meetings Run Too Long

Here are some questions to ask yourself to help keep the length of meetings under control:

• **Did we start on time?** Jim Davidson, author of *Effective Time Management* (Human Sciences Press), says a chief reason meetings run too long is that there is a lax attitude about starting on time. Every time someone drifts in late, he or she needs to be updated and the group loses its focus.

• **Did we accomplish what we set out to do?** Meetings will fill up the time allotted for them. Set a deadline — for example, one hour — but end the meeting if the agenda is completed early.

• **Did any item take too long?** "It's a fallacy to think decisions are better ones because everyone has participated with lengthy discourses," writes Davidson. "Lengthy discussion can cloud the central issue." Here's where setting a time limit helps. "When someone is taking a lot of time on one issue, you can ask for clarification and remind him of the time limit," he says.

• **Would forming an ad hoc committee have helped?** Writes Davidson, "When an item looks like it will take some time to consider, an ad hoc committee can be formed to study the matter and report back at the next meeting. This can save hours."

• **Could better preparation make things run smoother?** During a meeting, have someone keep a record of who is doing what in preparation for the next meeting. At the close of the meeting, have that person read the list to be sure everyone knows what they have been assigned.

Quick Tips

- **Talking and talking and talking.** At any meeting or training session, don't go beyond the scheduled time. In *Creative Training Techniques,* Bob Pike recommends that you deliver your practice talk in 10 percent less time than you've been allotted.

- **Good start.** Join a new team member on the first break of your team meeting. That action sends a clear signal, says *Enterprise* magazine. You show that you're interested and supportive.

- **No interruptions.** When a teammate is responding to a question, let that person finish answering without any interruption. Allow your coworker to keep his or her train of thought. The person may feel nervous to begin with. Asking questions before he or she finishes may intimidate your fellow team member.

- **Watch work flow.** Before you schedule a meeting, keep an eye on your teammates' work flow and the daily mail volume to gauge their availability, suggest Hedy and Les Abromovitz in *Bringing TQM on the QT to Your Organization* (SPC Press).

- **Bite your tongue.** If coworkers criticize you, bite your tongue and thank them for their good ideas and intentions, suggests *The George Odiorne Letter.* Even if you don't agree, accept that they meant well.

QUIZ

'DO I CONTRIBUTE TOO LITTLE IN MEETINGS?'

"Our team leader complains that some of us contribute little to meetings and let others carry the load. I try to participate, but nobody's really told me what I need to do."

— J.P.S., MACON, GA

You'll have to try harder! Begin by taking this test. It's adapted from one that Marion E. Haynes wrote for *Effective Meeting Skills* (Crisp Publications). Evaluate yourself by answering YES or NO.

	YES	NO
1. Do I usually know the purpose of the meetings I attend?	❏	❏
2. Do I understand my role?	❏	❏
3. Do I do my homework well in advance?	❏	❏
4. During the meeting do I engage in side conversations?	❏	❏
5. Do take phone calls during meetings?	❏	❏
6. When I'm not sure about something, do I ask questions?	❏	❏
7. Am I open to others' ideas?	❏	❏
8. Do I regularly participate in discussions?	❏	❏
9. Do I stick to the topic?	❏	❏
10. After a meeting, do I take the actions that the team has agreed upon?	❏	❏
11. Do I try to improve our meetings by giving feedback to teammates in attendance?	❏	❏
12. If teammates are absent, do I fill them in on what was discussed and decided?	❏	❏

YOUR MEETING CONTRIBUTION RATING: The desired answers to 4 and 5 are NO. You should have responded YES to all the others. Until you have a perfect score, you won't reach your full participation potential. If you're confused about the purpose of meetings and your role, arrange to speak with your team leader for clarification.

CHAPTER 10

SPARKING TEAM CREATIVITY

"Don't be afraid to go out on a limb. That's where the fruit is."
— ARTHUR F. LENEHAN

That half-empty glass is really half-full. Watch your team's ability to solve problems soar when you begin looking at the world from new perspectives.

A DOSE OF FUN CURES
CREATIVITY ROADBLOCKS

Your team functions well as a work unit, but nobody seems to be enjoying themselves. Creativity is at a low point as a result. How can you mix in a little pleasure with your labor?

Creative people always enjoy what they do, Sam Deep and Lyle Sussman assert in *Yes, You Can! 1105 Empowering Ideas for Life, Work, and Happiness* (Seminars by Sam Deep).

Here are a few of their suggestions for bringing pleasure to the workplace:

• Talk to some of the external and internal customers who benefit from your efforts. By realizing how much good work your team does, you'll feel recharged.

• Find new ways to perform old work. Take some risks and try to develop new, money-saving work habits.

• Watch for amusing events that occur in your team. Learn to laugh at yourselves.

• Post a funny but insightful team-related "Saying of the Month."

• Bring to your daily work the same vigor that you experience on days off.

• Begin to keep a daily work diary. Write in it all your successes and failures. When you run into a recurring problem, consult the diary to recall how you solved it a year or two ago.

INTERTEAM CREATIVITY

Not all problems can be solved by the members of one work team. In some instances, specialized expertise from other teams or departments is needed.

When you bring together the proper mix of coworkers, creative input can be converted into productive output in a short time.

Stephen R. Grossman, Bruce E. Rodgers, and Beverly F. Moore are the coauthors of *Innovation, Inc.: Unlocking Creativity in the Workplace* (Wordware Publishing). They've devised a format for all types of organizations.

• **Strive for creative sessions.** Their advice: Tap the creative powers of a group by organizing a brainstorming session. When planned and carried out correctly, these powwows can yield as many new ideas as you have time to consider.

When forming your group, choose people with different strengths and weaknesses. If you can, pull in people from all over the company.

A multitalented creative team, the authors indicate, needs personnel to fill three roles.

First, the *idea* people will generate most of the creative brainstorming input. The *facilitator* has the most complex task. Without suggesting ideas or discussing them it's that person's responsibility to keep the session flowing smoothly.

Finally, there's the *decision maker*. When a single team is deadlocked, the leader often serves as the tie breaker. Within an interteam structure, a different procedure may be needed.

One possibility: The decision maker might be the team member with the most seniority. No matter how the post is filled, the designated person could be the final arbiter.

As the brainstorming progresses, the *Innovation, Inc.* authors recommend, everyone should be free to let as many ideas fly as possible. A limit of 10 seconds per suggestion should be imposed. When everyone's input is combined, brainstorming on one topic can be completed in 10 or 15 minutes.

- **Evaluate ideas.** Evaluation represents the second stage. Here, ideas are refined and converted into viable solutions. Such factors as time, technology, money, and people are all considered. Flaws also should be studied and discussed.

If the facilitator has written down the ideas, focus on those that interest you the most.

"Choose the concepts that you find interesting, provocative, or exciting," the authors suggest. "At this point, you don't have to know how to make the idea work. You and the group will get to the practical decisions later."

- **Do it again.** Now repeat the entire process. This time, hone in on hard-cash matters. For instance, let's say that you've determined that implementing an idea will require a 25 percent increase in your advertising budget. Where will the money come from?

When the team can't agree on a solution, the decision maker often has the last word. The exceptions might be projects that require further reviews and approvals. For such cases, team representatives could make a presentation to management.

WHISTLE WHILE YOU WORK?

The seven dwarfs may have been right.

Whistling while you work to the beat of a Walkman radio headset has become part of some employees' routines.

Walkmans have jumped from the heads of joggers to office and plant workers, according to *The Wall Street Journal*.

Employers note the up and down sides of these personal, on-the-job concerts:

PROS:

• Music can promote concentration by helping employees tune out noise around them and tune into their tasks. "I think it keeps their minds off the stress, and it does help improve quality," says David Benjamin, vice president of regional processing for Banc One in Columbus, Ohio.

• Research studies show that assembly-line workers who wear Walkmans on the job have equal work quality as those who don't, but experience higher job satisfaction.

• Music's rhythm encourages a rhythm in employees' work, helping them to keep a consistently productive pace.

CONS:

• In a team environment, Walkmans can stall communication among members.

• Some employers see music as a distraction that will hurt productivity. "You have too many people to talk to and too many things to do at one time," says Raul Ramos, creative director of B-R-C Marketing in Dayton, Ohio.

• Being "plugged in" to a Walkman can send out the message that employees do not want to be disturbed and are not interested in working as team players.

'SHAPE' TEAM MEETINGS TO OPEN
CREATIVE DIALOGUE

Need a catalyst to get your next team meeting off to a great start?

Try this activity demonstrated at the 16th Annual Association for Quality and Participation Conference.

At the start of the meeting, give each member of your team a piece of pipe cleaner. Then ask members to mold the pipe cleaners into a shape that they feel represents the way the team is functioning today. Finally, have each member, in turn, explain what his or her design says about the team.

Example: One participant shaped her pipe cleaner into a triangle, explaining that her team structure was still very hierarchical, with all the power in the hands of a few people at the top, while most of the work was done by several people at the bottom. Another individual shaped his pipe cleaner into an arrow with a dot at the beginning, signifying that his team had only just begun its teamwork effort and still had a long road to follow in pursuit of success.

This exercise, introduced by conference presenters Diane Andrews and James Reed of Texas Instruments Defense Group, is sure to bring out the creativity in your team's members, while sparking introspective team discussion. *But*: Do not judge anyone's creation as right or wrong.

'WRITING-TO-LEARN' METHODS
STIMULATE CREATIVITY

Team "brainstorming" meetings can sometimes get out of control, degenerating into shouting matches.

Julie S. Hile, president of The Training Connection in Oxford, Ohio, suggests an alternative idea-swapping method in

Training & Development. It's called "writing-to-learn" (WTL) and can be used for training, creativity-building, problem solving, or almost any other form of team communication.

Hile lists 10 exercises that are part of the WTL process:

- **Participant goals.** The facilitator asks team members to read the workshop objectives and write what they hope to accomplish, numbering them in order of importance.

- **Written brainstorming.** Participants have one minute to brainstorm — in writing — on a given topic. By drawing circles around parts of their statements, they remind themselves to do some serious thinking about certain ideas.

- **Miscellaneous notes and questions.** Anything goes here. Teammates put on paper whatever comes into their minds that relates to the designated topic.

- **Definitions.** Team members write their own definitions of various terms. Later, they'll be asked to review and revise them. Writing rather than memorizing these definitions forces members to think for themselves.

- **Dialoguing.** Two teammates fold a sheet of paper vertically in half. One teammate writes something about the topic on one side of the paper. The second person then responds to this thought on the other side of the page. As the process continues, teammates become more comfortable sharing their thoughts.

- **Silent discussion.** The facilitator writes several words on the flip chart. They're designed to elicit responses, which the trainees add to the chart. This silent exchange of written ideas encourages participants to carefully consider their thoughts instead of blurting them out as often happens in group discussions.

- **Time out.** When the session becomes tense or bogs down, everyone writes about their general thoughts at a slower pace. It's similar to the disciplinary technique used with young children.

- **Directions.** Each team member writes six separate sets of instructions for a task that he or she has mastered. The would-be readers are designated as a child, a teammate, a parent, the boss, an expert in the field, and a novice.

- **Participants' menu.** The menu is a list of questions each participant makes about new procedures or skills. By writing and sharing questions, each teammate learns how much he or she knows about the topic and how to fill in the gaps of the personal learning process.

- **Graffiti.** In this final exercise, members scribble down whatever they want. This exercise often reveals attitudes and knowledge levels.

"Writing-to-learn gets people to move ideas from inside their heads to the outside," Hile explains. "Once they write them down, they're less protective and defensive about what they think and believe."

No joke: Humor works!

For team leaders: true or false?

1. Using humor with your team diminishes your authority.

2. Laughing with coworkers is inappropriate.

3. Humor and a team's success aren't related.

Any true answers? If so, you are probably one of the countless team leaders who are overlooking a powerful leadership tool.

"Used appropriately, humor can help motivate, relax, and inspire team members to top achievement," says Esther Blumenfeld, coauthor (with Lynne Alpern) of the book *Humor at Work* (Peach Tree Publishers).

Constructive humor can help create a positive team atmosphere, spice up creative brainstorming sessions, and add color to potentially dull memos and meetings.

Still not convinced? "Ask yourself, what do a close-knit family, a championship team, and a thriving business organization have in common?" says author Bob Ross in his book *That's a Good One!* (Avant Books): "First and foremost, the members enjoy being together, laughing, playing, and having fun making things happen. And the best of the winning groups are those in which the leaders are considered members of the team."

No one is advocating that as a team leader you become an entertainer to be laughed at rather than with, or that you become so permissive that you lose the respect of your team. But you should consider humor as one additional way to communicate with your team.

What can humor do for you? It can strengthen your team by:

1. Lessening tension. J. Burton Gruber, of Expedite, Inc., had a contest for his team of accountants at the height of tax season. A bottle of champagne went to the person with the best suggestions about "what to do" with a tax form. Some suggestions: 1. Fold them and see which one is properly weighed to fly. 2. Prop a wobbly chair. 3. Envy it. The contest broke some of the stress of working long hours on tight deadlines.

2. Helping send a message. A team had been going through an unproductive period. At one meeting, the leader asked the team to stand up and look under their chairs. Taped underneath was a nickel. What did it prove? After a few minutes, a team member accurately summed up the message. "It proves we can't sit on our duffs and even earn a nickel." The team leader had gotten their attention, pointed out a problem, and made her point.

3. Building teamwork. "An effective leader can increase

cohesiveness by humorously focusing on the competitive relationship with other groups within the organization, with another company, or with foreign competition," says Esther Blumenfeld. An American plant foreman told this joke to his crew: "One thing about asking Europeans to buy as many products from us as we buy from them: it lets you know who your friends *were.*"

4. Keeping team members' attention. Sitting in a dark room watching a complex presentation can be a nap waiting to happen. A sales team leader slips in an occasional funny or incongruous slide: "Here's the graph of projected industry growth for the next five years ... here's a pie of foreign competition ... here's my dog at the beach last summer."

There are an endless number of other contributions humor can make to your team. But most of all, don't forget the most obvious: humor makes us happy. Consider the words of psychologist William James: "We don't laugh because we're happy — we're happy because we laugh."

Now start sharing that smile with the members of your team!

TRY THIS!

Ready for some fun? Try this advice from the experts:

- *Use humor that fits you.* Think: "What makes me laugh?"
- *Don't do stand-up comedy.*
- *Start slowly.* Wear a funny lapel pin or post funny signs.
- *Have humor rituals,* such as a "funny quote of the day" or a "funny customer experience."
- *Keep a "first-aid kit."* Stock it with things that make you laugh: funny cartoons, greeting cards, comedy tapes. Share them with your team.

- *Laugh at yourself.* Set the tone by taking your job seriously and yourself lightly.

- *Laugh often.* Keep in mind the words of humorist Erma Bombeck: "When humor goes, there goes civilization.

BOSSES LIKE HUMOR, TOO

Here's another good reason to inject more humor in the workplace: bosses like it!

In a survey by Accountemps, the temporary personnel service, executives were asked, *"Do people with a sense of humor do better, the same as, or worse at their jobs than those with little or no sense of humor?"* Their responses: *Better:* 96%; *Same:* 3%; *Worse:* 0%; *Don't know:* 1%.

"Those who laugh frequently tend to be better communicators and make better team players," says Robert Half, founder of Accountemps. "They also realize humor is vital in reducing stress."

AT&T'S 'KILLER' HUMOR TEAM

Everyone was getting just a little too serious around the New Jersey billing operations office, so AT&T Associate Manager Charlie Neagoy took matters into his own hands.

He formed a humor team.

"At AT&T work teams are formed to tackle all sorts of problems," says Neagoy. "We weren't sure how management would feel about a humor team, but we've been pleasantly surprised."

The team, known as BOFFO (Billing Operations for Fun Organization) is made up of five members. Neagoy was chosen as the group's leader.

The team meets regularly to develop innovative ways to inject fun and humor in their workplace.

During its first six months, the team sponsored a pumpkin-carving contest and a white-water rafting race. But its most popular event has been "Who Killed Bill?" a murder mystery carried out over AT&T's e-mail system.

"We created a fictional story in which the top executive of the world's largest telecommunications company was killed off," says Neagoy. "We sent out clues every day over the e-mail system. The first three sleuths to correctly solve the murder won prizes."

The murder mystery earned the team an "Innovation Award" from management.

But what was most gratifying, says Neagoy, was "the number of employees who followed the clues and tried to solve the mystery. Even managers would stop us in the halls and tell us, 'We're behind this all the way.' They were having fun — and that's exactly what the humor team set out to accomplish."

If you're thinking of launching a humor team, Neagoy suggests: "Keep it fun and informal. Remember, *planning* to have fun should be fun, too."

SERIOUSLY, NOW, A LITTLE HUMOR HELPS

Joel Goodman is serious about humor.

He is the director of The HUMOR Project in Saratoga Springs, New York, as well as a popular speaker, consultant and workshop leader. Goodman has addressed more than 500,000 people, including educators, managers, team members and team leaders at companies like IBM and AT&T, on the link between humor, creativity, and communication.

We shared a few laughs — and some serious talk — with Goodman at The HUMOR Project's Annual International Conference on Humor and Creativity.

Q: In your workshop you say, "Take your job seriously, but yourself lightly." Isn't that a contradiction?

A: Not at all. Take seriously your goals, roles, and missions in life, but it's important to take yourself lightly. Many people agree laughter is the best medicine, but they question the use of humor in the serious world of business.

The bottom line doesn't takes precedence over the funny line. The two lines go together.

Q: What contribution does humor make in the workplace?

A: Humor is a very good way of managing stress. If people can be more effective in responding to stress, then they're going to be more productive and healthier.

Q: What about work teams? Why should team leaders be serious about humor?

A: In teams, relationships are important. And humor is a great way of building relationships. We look at Victor Borge's notion that laughter is the shortest distance between two people. For team leaders, it's a way of motivating people, making the team a more enjoyable environment. When used constructively, humor maximizes the effectiveness of a team.

Q: What about the team leader who says, "Great, but I'm just not good at telling jokes?"

A: One of the biggest misconceptions is that, to be humorous, you have to be a joke teller. Although joke-telling is one way to transmit humor, it's not the only way.

Q: Starting right now, how can team leaders bring some humor into their work situations?

A: Try a bulletin board of cartoons that poke some fun at some serious issue confronting the team. Use a lighthearted quote at a meeting. Put a sign on your desk that invites laugher.

Q: What else?

A: Laugh at yourself. Remember what John F. Kennedy said: "There are three things which are real: God, human folly, and laughter. The first two are beyond our comprehension. So we must do what we can with the third."

WHY EVERYONE WITH AN IDEA IS 'IMPORTANT'

The best and most original ideas don't always come from the most articulate or most experienced team members. Look around and you'll find winning ideas from unlikely sources.

Robert J. Doyle and Paul I. Doyle relate the experience of one unidentified company in *Gain Management: A System for Building Teamwork, Productivity & Profitability Throughout Your Organization* (AMACOM).

For 20 years, the company had a successful program for sharing with team members savings gained from their ideas. As part of a cost-reduction campaign, management urged workers to submit more top-quality ideas than ever before.

After the announcement was made, a quiet and modest electrician hesitantly walked over to his manager and said:

"I've had this idea about the grinding machine controls for the past five years. I think it could save as much as $50,000 a year in costs and downtime. I haven't turned it in before because it's such a big change. But now, with this new push, maybe I should. What do you think?"

The manager encouraged the electrician and helped him to put his proposal in writing. After the new controls were approved and in operation, they resulted in first-year savings of $57,000.

The electrician said he hadn't spoken up sooner because he'd always assumed "big" ideas came from "important" people.

Are any of your fellow team members working under the misconception that they aren't "important?"

CHEER TEAM SPIRIT ALONG

Winning sports teams aren't the only teams that should celebrate now and then. You can apply the same type of energy and excitement to your work team. Here's how:

• **Share the spotlight.** When the team has completed a difficult task, congratulate everyone, not just the "star player." Your goal was reached as a team, so remember to celebrate as one.

• **Spread the feeling.** Motivate your teammates by creating a positive and energetic mood. Peer influence can be a strong force within a team and can bring about positive results.

• **Enjoy your teammates' company.** Encourage camaraderie by getting together outside of work. Meet for a casual dinner or backyard barbecue.

• **Keep in touch.** Avoid using the grapevine as a means of communication. Inevitably, someone will be left out, and the team will become splintered into cliques. A spirited team is also one that is productive. Keep up the team spirit and win the productivity game!

CREATING A CREATIVE TEAM ENVIRONMENT

Here's a list of ways to build a creative work environment, compiled by Arthur G. VanGundy, author of *Managing Group Creativity* (American Management Association):

- **Encourage open expression of ideas.** Team leaders must reward efforts to be innovative and create a team atmosphere that at least gives new ideas a fair hearing. It's a leader's task to get everybody to open up.

- **Accept divergent ideas.** A work team that respects differences among its members is going to accomplish much more than any think-alike group.

- **Assist in developing ideas.** When a team member comes up with a good idea but can't fully refine it, all team members should "pitch in" with questions and suggestions to help the idea's originator feel supported and to encourage further creative thinking.

- **Provide time for individual efforts.** As vital as teamwork is in any organization, people often need time alone to devise creative solutions. Set aside that time before any group action is made final.

- **Furnish opportunities for personal growth.** At any job level, workers find that old ways of doing things eventually become obsolete. They need to be "reborn" every so often in order to acquire additional knowledge. Think of innovative techniques to tackle team problems.

Quick Tips

- **Idea file.** Keep an active file of ideas collected from colleagues and even competitors. These tips can spur creative thinking about your work practices. Pull out the file and look over the ideas from time to time.

- **But on our team?** Laughter is fun and all, but does it belong in the team environment? Of course it does, say Esther Blumenfeld and Lynne Alpern, authors of *The Smile Connection: How to Use Humor in Dealing With People* (Prentice Hall). The authors told *Woman* magazine that humor in teams "helps gain trust and makes others more receptive to your ideas."

- **Time blockers.** You can spur creativity by eliminating your wristwatch, suggests *Men's Fitness*. Instead of looking at your watch ever few minutes, check your computer clock as needed. You'll forget about clock time and lose yourself in your creative thoughts.

- **Turn bad days around.** When a bad day interferes with your ability to think creatively, bend a coworker's ear about what's bugging you or treat yourself to something special, like an ice cream cone during coffee break, suggests author Bruce A. Baldwin in *All in Your Head* (Warner Books).

- **Fun all along the way.** "The joy of life should never be postponed for the chance of eventual success, says entrepreneur Jack Nadel: "Each step along the way must bring some form of gratification. No one has a passport that tells him or her how long he or she will live. The pursuit of success should be as much fun as achieving it."

GAUGE YOUR TEAM'S 'INNOVATION QUOTIENT'

"The status quo isn't enough for our team. We want to be known for our creativity. How can we rate how we rank as innovators?"

— P.D.Y., MADISON, WI

Have team members gauge their "innovation quotient." This measurement was devised by Twyla Dell, author of *An Honest Day's Work* (Crisp Publications), as part of an "IQ" concept. The test that follows is based on one in her book. After each question, give yourself a 3 for ALWAYS; 2 for SOMETIMES; 1 for ONCE IN A WHILE; and 0 for NEVER.

SCORE

1. Can you detect problems and trends that aren't visible on the surface? _____

2. Do you look for opportunities to solve problems? _____

3. Do you challenge biases and preconceived beliefs? _____

4. Can you spot emerging trends that will affect your team? _____

5. Do you seek out ideas from other fields that can be incorporated into your team efforts? _____

6. Do you look beyond statistics for human needs? _____

7. In general, are you fascinated by the future? _____

8. Through listening and feedback, do you welcome ideas that may be better than yours? _____

9. Do you seek out other innovative thinkers? _____

10. Do you read books and magazines that deal with innovation both in general and in your field? _____

Total _____

YOUR CREATIVITY IQ: With a score of 27 to 30, "we'll see your name in lights someday," Dell says. At 21 to 26, you're on the verge of becoming a "discoverer." A total of 18 to 20 labels you as "a good support person." With a lower score, "you're a maintainer and conservator of the past whose talents seem to lie in other areas."